Practical Lua 5 Programming

Explore Lua's programming capabilities with 100+ sample demonstrations and programs

Brynna Kevar

Published by: GitforGits

Publisher: Sonal Dhandre

www.gitforgits.com

support@gitforgits.com

Printed in India

First Printing: December 2024

ISBN: 978-81-984316-6-0

Cover Design by: Kitten Publishing

Prologue

Why should one learn Lua programming? I've always been drawn to Lua's simplicity and elegance. From rapid scripting chores to constructing full-scale web apps, its minimal footprint and simplicity of embedding make it the perfect solution for a variety of projects. I intended to write a book guiding you actively, hands-on with Lua. From what I know, Lua's adaptability helps you to swiftly address actual problems and its simple architecture keeps you concentrated on what really counts: developing code that works.

I discuss in this book my own exploits and useful lessons with Lua 5. You will accompany me as I create a Linux development environment, write your first Lua script, and investigate the key language features including dynamic typing, tables, and functions. The best approach to grasp the possibilities of code is, in my opinion, seeing it in use. More sophisticated subjects such metatables, closures, and coroutines will come up as you proceed. These ideas will enable you to produce maintainable, powerful modular, reusable code.

Working with Lua's inherent features will allow me to additionally show you how to perform regular chores including data parsing and file management. We'll start with installing and managing modules using LuaRocks, then you'll see personally how to neatly, self-containedly package your code. You will find useful examples that clearly show either building web apps with the Lapis framework or incorporating Lua into JavaScript and Python projects.

When we go through this, I want you to remember that every example is a stepping stone to creating your own projects. I concentrate on what counts—useable skills you can expand and adapt. My goal is to enable you to make efficient use of Lua so that you will have a strong grasp of its fundamental ideas and will be able to enjoy the process of developing dynamic, useful applications. I eagerly offer these observations since I personally know how transforming a well-written Lua script can be. Every chapter, when you flip the pages, is meant to build on the one before it. This book addresses most of the requirements to start you with Lua programming.

For those ready to investigate and maximize Lua's powers, this book is not a mastery guide but rather you can use it to test your essentials of Lua.

Content

Preface

If you're into Lua programming, "Practical Lua 5 Programming" is a must-read. It's a hands-on book that'll help you get up and running quickly. It's got clear, step-by-step examples that'll walk you through everything from setting up your development environment to building dynamic web applications and embedding Lua in other programming languages. Every chapter starts with an essential concept and then gives you some practical exercises to help you learn it. You'll see how powerful Lua can be as you work through problems and get immediate results. You'll start with the basics, like installing Lua on Linux, writing your first script, and learning the core language features like variables, data types, tables, functions, and control structures. And it gets even better—you'll dive into advanced stuff like metatables, coroutines, and closures. This is where you'll learn how to make flexible, modular code. The book also covers important stuff like file handling, using LuaRocks to manage your packages, and creating your own custom modules.

The book also takes you through web development using Lapis framework, demonstrating routing, template rendering, session management, and deploying applications. You'll also see how Lua can be embedded in JavaScript and Python applications, enabling you to leverage Lua's speed and efficiency in varied environments. Whether you're building scripts, web applications, or integrating Lua with other languages, this book gives you the tools and insights you need to get started confidently with Lua programming.

In this book you will learn to:

- Install and configure Lua on Linux for efficient scripting.
- Make use of Lua's dynamic typing, tables, and control structures.
- Create and work around metatables, closures, and coroutines for modular code.
- Apply file I/O and data parsing to manage persistent data.
- Use LuaRocks to install, update, and manage custom modules.
- Build web apps with Lapis using routing and session management.
- Embed Lua in JavaScript and Python to boost performance.
- Integrate HTTP, JSON, and APIs for system data exchange.
- Implement middleware and session tracking for secure apps.
- Deploy Lua apps with configuration and performance monitoring.

GitforGits

Prerequisites

Whether you're building scripts, web applications, or integrating Lua with other languages, this book is a go-to guide for every programmer and application developer to get started with Lua.

Codes Usage

Are you in need of some helpful code examples to assist you in your programming and documentation? Look no further! Our book offers a wealth of supplemental material, including code examples and exercises.

Not only is this book here to aid you in getting your job done, but you have our permission to use the example code in your programs and documentation. However, please note that if you are reproducing a significant portion of the code, we do require you to contact us for permission.

But don't worry, using several chunks of code from this book in your program or answering a question by citing our book and quoting example code does not require permission. But if you do choose to give credit, an attribution typically includes the title, author, publisher, and ISBN. For example, "Practical Lua 5 Programming by Brynna Kevar".

If you are unsure whether your intended use of the code examples falls under fair use or the permissions outlined above, please do not hesitate to reach out to us at support@gitforgits.com.

We are happy to assist and clarify any concerns.

Acknowledgement

I owe a tremendous debt of gratitude to GitforGits, for their unflagging enthusiasm and wise counsel throughout the entire process of writing this book. Their knowledge and careful editing helped make sure the piece was useful for people of all reading levels and comprehension skills. In addition, I'd like to thank everyone involved in the publishing process for their efforts in making this book a reality. Their efforts, from copyediting to advertising, made the project what it is today.

Finally, I'd like to express my gratitude to everyone who has shown me unconditional love and encouragement throughout my life. Their support was crucial to the completion of this book. I appreciate your help with this endeavour and your continued interest in my career.

Chapter 1: Getting Started with Lua 5

Overview

Let us start our Lua journey with the first part. The first thing we do is carefully set up our Linux environment and install the Lua interpreter. We make sure that every detail is taken care of by following step-by-step instructions to set up system variables and check our installation. As you write our first Lua script, the change from installing to coding goes smoothly. This gives you immediate feedback and a solid base for our Lua learning journey. You'll be ready for a deeper look into Lua after this first step.

After setting up Lua, you look at its core syntax and get to know its unique language constructs. We get to use variables, data types, expressions, and control structures as you learn them, which makes you want to try new things. Your understanding will be strengthened by clear, useful examples that show how Lua's syntax is different from other programming languages. With each new thing you learn, our skills get better.

In the last part of this chapter, you use Lua's interactive REPL to try out code fragments and do experiments right away. We should use the REPL as a sandbox to test our ideas and get a better grasp on Lua concepts. We develop a habit of learning and exploring things over and over again by using this interactive method. This gets you ready for more advanced topics later on in our Lua journey. That makes you feel better.

Setting up Environment

Lua is a lightweight scripting language that's both efficient and easy to embed in apps. You'll see that the interpreter not only executes scripts but also provides an interactive shell where you can test snippets of code instantly. The interpreter gives you immediate feedback, which is invaluable as you explore Lua's syntax and core concepts. We can experiment as much as you want in the interactive shell, which will help you get a better handle on things before moving on to the harder topics.

Installing Lua

Using Package Manager

If you prefer a quick and simple installation, you can install Lua directly from our Linux distribution's package repositories. For example, on Debian-based systems like Ubuntu, open our terminal and run:

```
sudo apt update
sudo apt install lua5.4
```

These commands update our package list and install Lua version 5.4 from the repository. Should you be using Fedora, you might run:

```
sudo dnf install lua
```

Or, on CentOS, you can use:

```
sudo yum install lua
```

Each of these commands installs the Lua interpreter along with any required libraries, providing you with a ready-to-use environment for scripting.

Installing Lua from Source

If you choose to build Lua from source for customization or to obtain a specific version, you start by downloading the source code from the official Lua website. We go onto the terminal and execute:

```
cd /tmp
wget https://www.lua.org/ftp/lua-5.4.4.tar.gz
tar -xzvf lua-5.4.4.tar.gz
cd lua-5.4.4
make linux test
```

Here, you download the Lua tarball, extract its contents, compile the source using the provided Makefile, and run tests to verify the build. Once you have confirmed that everything works correctly, you install Lua by running:

```
sudo make install
```

The above command copies the Lua binaries to standard directories (typically **/usr/local/bin**). With this, you can tailor the build process to suit our requirements.

Configuring Environment Variables

Most package managers place Lua in a directory that is already included in our **PATH**, but if you built Lua from source or installed it in a custom directory, you will need to update our environment variables manually.

To update the **PATH**, open our shell configuration file. If you are using Bash, edit the **~/.bashrc** file:

```
nano ~/.bashrc
```

At the end of the file, add the following line, replacing **/usr/local/bin** with the correct directory if necessary:

```
export PATH=$PATH:/usr/local/bin
```

After saving our changes, apply them by running:

```
source ~/.bashrc
```

This reloads our configuration and our terminal recognizes the directory where Lua is installed. We can also verify that the Lua executable is in our **PATH** by typing:

```
echo $PATH
```

You ned to check the output to confirm that the directory **/usr/local/bin** (or our custom directory) is included. This step confirms that every time you run a Lua command, our system locates the correct executable.

Verifying Installation

Checking Lua Version

Once Lua is installed and our environment is configured, verify the installation by checking the Lua version. In our terminal, type:

```
lua -v
```

The terminal should display version information similar to:

```
Lua 5.4.4  Copyright (C) 1994-2022 Lua.org, PUC-Rio
```

The version number confirms that Lua is installed correctly and that the system can locate the interpreter.

Running Interactive Lua Shell

Next, you test the interactive mode by launching the Lua shell. In our terminal, type:

```
lua
```

A prompt appears, typically represented by the character **>**, indicating that you can now enter Lua commands interactively. For example, you try:

```
print("Hello, Lua!")
```

After pressing Enter, the interpreter displays:

```
Hello, Lua!
```

This immediate feedback assures you that the Lua environment is functioning as expected. We exit the interactive shell by pressing **`Ctrl+D`** or by typing:

```
os.exit()
```

Testing Basic Lua Commands

To further familiarize yourself with the interpreter, you experiment with additional Lua commands. Begin with a simple arithmetic operation by typing:

```
print(5 + 10)
```

The expected output is:

```
15
```

Next, assign a value to a variable and display it:

```
message = "Lua is fun!"
print(message)
```

The interpreter should output:

```
Lua is fun!
```

This means that the basic Lua operations are running smoothly. You'll get to try out the language's core functions and see how practical it is.

Writing First Lua Script

Creating Script

You begin by opening our preferred text editor. If you enjoy a command-line interface, you might use nano or vim. For instance, you type:

```
nano hello.lua
```

This command opens nano and creates a file named hello.lua if it does not already exist. The file you create will hold our Lua script, which will soon output a simple message to confirm that everything is working as expected.

Writing Code

Within the text editor, you write a straightforward Lua script. The primary goal here is to print a message to the terminal, so in our hello.lua file, you add the following code:

```
-- hello.lua
print("Hello, Lua!")
```

This script begins with a comment, indicated by the double hyphen, which helps you document the purpose of our code. The **`print`** function is one of Lua's most basic commands; it outputs the text enclosed in quotes to the terminal.

Saving and Running Script

After you have written the code, you save our file. In nano, you press Ctrl+O to write out the file and then Ctrl+X to exit. If you are using vim, you would press Esc followed by typing **`:wq`** to save and exit. And then, you execute the script with:

```
lua hello.lua
```

This command instructs the Lua interpreter to execute the code contained in hello.lua. When you press Enter, the interpreter processes the script and outputs the text specified by the print function. We watch the terminal to see "Hello, Lua!" appear, confirming that the script has executed successfully.

Validating Script Execution

The immediate display of "Hello, Lua!" on our terminal serves as a confirmation that our Lua script has been executed correctly. The process of writing a file, saving it, and then executing it allows you to validate each step of our workflow. If the expected output does not appear, you know to revisit our code for possible syntax errors or misconfigurations in the file. This method of checking our work through direct feedback from the Lua interpreter is a valuable practice that reinforces our understanding of how Lua code is interpreted and executed on a Linux system.

As you continue to explore Lua, you will build on this fundamental workflow, and dive more into the complexity of scripts while always ensuring that you can verify the success of each task through immediate, observable output.

Understanding Lua Syntax

To explore, let us recall the sample program we wrote earlier:

```
-- hello.lua
print("Hello, Lua!")
```

This program uses the **`print`** function to output a string literal to the terminal. The string **`"Hello, Lua!"`** is a simple example of a data type in Lua. By starting with this example, you can now expand our understanding to include how variables store values, how different data types interact, and how operators perform calculations and comparisons.

Variables in Lua

In Lua, you do not need to declare the type of a variable before using it. We simply assign a value to a name, and Lua manages the type dynamically. Variables allow you to store and manipulate data.

For instance, you can modify the sample program by introducing a variable to hold our greeting message:

```
-- hello_with_variable.lua
greeting = "Hello, Lua!"
print(greeting)
```

In this code, **`greeting`** is a variable that holds the string value **`"Hello, Lua!"`**. We can later change the value stored in **`greeting`** without worrying about its type. This flexibility is one of Lua's strengths and encourages experimentation. We might try modifying the variable by appending more text or by using it in different contexts within our scripts.

Data Types in Lua

Lua also supports several fundamental data types that you will frequently use:

String

A sequence of characters enclosed in quotes. In the sample programs above, **`"Hello, Lua!"`** is a string.

Number

Lua treats numbers in a straightforward way, whether they are integers or floating-point values. For example:

```
value = 42
```

```
pi = 3.14159
print("The value is", value)
print("The value of pi is", pi)
```

Boolean

Represents truth values with **true** and **false**. We can use booleans to control the flow of our program.

Nil

Thius represents the absence of a useful value. When a variable has not been assigned a meaningful value, it can be **nil**.

You can combine these types in various ways. For example, you might create a script that demonstrates how variables of different types can be printed and manipulated:

```
-- data_types_demo.lua
name = "Lua Programmer"      -- string
age = 25                     -- number
is_active = true             -- boolean
print("Name:", name)
print("Age:", age)
print("Active Status:", is_active)
```

If you run this script, it'll print out the values stored in the variables, showing you how Lua handles each data type. We can experiment with different assignments and print statements to see how Lua converts and displays each type.

Operators in Lua

The operators in Lua allow you to perform arithmetic, relational, and logical operations. Here are some basic categories of operators you will encounter:

Arithmetic Operators

The Lua supports standard arithmetic operators such as addition (**+**), subtraction (**-**), multiplication (*****), division (**/**), and modulus (**%**). For example, you can perform arithmetic calculations like this:

```
-- arithmetic_demo.lua
a = 10
b = 3
sum = a + b
difference = a - b
product = a * b
quotient = a / b
remainder = a % b
print("Sum:", sum)                    -- 13
print("Difference:", difference)      -- 7
print("Product:", product)            -- 30
print("Quotient:", quotient)          -- 3.3333333333333
print("Remainder:", remainder)        -- 1
```

Relational Operators

The relational operators compare two values and return a boolean result. These include equality (**==**), inequality (**~=**), greater than (**>**), less than (**<**), greater than or equal to (**>=**), and less than or equal to (**<=**). For example:

```
-- relational_demo.lua
x = 15
y = 20
print("x equals y:", x == y)
print("x not equal to y:", x ~= y)
print("x is less than y:", x < y)
print("x is greater than y:", x > y)
```

Logical Operators

There are logical operators such as **and**, **or**, and **not** allow you to combine or invert boolean values. They are often used in control structures to manage the flow of our program. For instance:

```
-- logical_demo.lua
a = true
b = false
result_and = a and b
result_or = a or b
result_not = not a
print("a and b:", result_and)
print("a or b:", result_or)
print("not a:", result_not)
```

These operators enable you to create conditions that determine how our script should proceed based on the values of variables.

Combining Variables, Data Types, and Operators

To really get a handle on this, you can create a script that mixes variables, different data types, and operators as below:

```
-- syntax_example.lua
-- Define variables of different data types
name = "Lua Learner"          -- string
year_started = 2020           -- number
current_year = 2025           -- number
active = true                 -- boolean
-- Calculate the number of years of experience
experience = current_year - year_started
-- Create a personalized message using string concatenation
and arithmetic
message = "Hello, " .. name .. "! You have been learning Lua
for " .. experience .. " years."
print(message)
```

Here, in this example, you declare a bunch of variables with different data types, like strings, numbers, and booleans. We use the subtraction operator to figure out the number of years of experience and the concatenation operator (..) to combine strings with the computed value. When you run this script, it should show a complete sentence that reflects the variables' values and shows how arithmetic and string concatenation work together.

Interactive Sessions with REPL

Now, let's take a look at the power of the interactive Lua interpreter. It's also called the REPL, short for read-eval-print loop. With this, you now have a solid foundation in writing and running Lua scripts from files. The REPL gives you the ability to do experiments directly in our Linux terminal. This cool dynamic environment lets you type in commands one at a time and see the results right away. That makes it a breeze to test out new ideas, debug code and explore Lua's features in real-time. It'll help you build confidence by letting you interact with Lua without the hassle of creating and saving a script file each time.

Launching Interactive Shell

To start the REPL, type:

```
lua
```

Once you press Enter, you will see a prompt that typically looks like this:

markdown

```
>
```

This prompt indicates that Lua is ready to accept commands. We can now enter Lua code directly and see instant output. For example, type the following command:

```
print("Welcome to the Lua REPL!")
```

After pressing Enter, you should see:

css

```
Welcome to the Lua REPL!
```

This immediate display confirms that the interpreter is functioning and that you can now experiment with Lua interactively.

Testing Simple Scripts

In the REPL, you can test snippets of code without writing a complete script as shown in the below:

```
5 + 10
```

The REPL will immediately output:

```
15
```

You can assign values to variables interactively, too. For example, type:

```
x = 42
print(x)
```

After you press Enter, you will see:

```
42
```

This process helps you validate our understanding of basic syntax as you see the result of each command instantly.

Experimenting with Lua Features

The interactive shell is an excellent tool for exploring different Lua features. We can define functions, work with tables, and even test control structures without needing to commit to a full script.

For instance, try creating a simple function:

```
function greet(name)
    return "Hello, " .. name .. "!"
end
print(greet("Explorer"))
```

This command creates a function that concatenates a greeting message and then prints the result. We should see:

```
Hello, Explorer!
```

Another area to explore is loops. Experiment with a simple loop to iterate over a sequence of numbers:

```
for i = 1, 5 do
    print("Iteration:", i)
```

```
end
```

The REPL will execute the loop and output a line for each iteration, letting you verify the logic immediately. Such experiments reinforce our understanding of Lua's control structures and help you build a more intuitive grasp of the language.

Exploring Real-time Feedback

One of the greatest advantages of using the REPL is the real-time feedback it provides. As soon as you enter a command, Lua evaluates it and displays the result. This instant response lets you quickly identify errors or unintended behavior.

For example, if you mistype a command:

```
prit("Typo example")
```

Lua will return an error message indicating the issue. We can immediately correct the mistake and re-run the command. This iterative process enables you to learn from errors and make adjustments without delay. The interactive session becomes a live conversation with the interpreter, where each command you type refines our understanding of Lua's syntax and behavior.

You can also inspect data structures on the fly. If you create a table and want to check its contents, try:

```
myTable = { "apple", "banana", "cherry" }
for index, value in ipairs(myTable) do
    print(index, value)
end
```

The REPL displays the index-value pairs immediately, providing a clear view of how Lua organizes data in tables.

When you are finished experimenting, you can exit the REPL by pressing Ctrl+D on our keyboard, or by typing:

```
os.exit()
```

This command gracefully terminates the session and returns you to our Linux terminal. The simplicity of starting and stopping the REPL makes it a flexible tool that you can use frequently without worrying about managing complex files or processes.

Summary

To quickly go over what we've learned, you started learning Lua by setting up our Linux environment and installing the Lua interpreter in two different ways: through the package manager and from source code. After setting up environment variables and making sure the interpreter could be reached, you checked the Lua version to make sure the installation was complete. We made our first Lua script that printed a greeting message.

Then you learned the basics of Lua syntax by looking at how variables, data types, and operators worked in simple programs. We saw how string literals, numbers, booleans, and math operations worked together to get the results you wanted. In addition, you used the interactive Lua interpreter session (called the REPL) to play around with bits of code and get feedback right away. We learned a lot about Lua in this chapter by going through the whole process, from installing it to experimenting with it in real time.

CHAPTER 2: LUA DATA STRUCTURES AND VARIABLES

Overview

Here we are at chapter 2. In this chapter, you will learn about the basics of Lua by working with variables and data types that our scripts are built on. We will learn how to work with strings, numbers, booleans, and nil, as well as how to declare and assign variables on the fly. We will also learn how these types of data work together in expressions and how to use operators to do basic math and logic.

Then you'll learn about how to use tables in a variety of ways, such as arrays and dictionaries to organize groups of data effectively. We will learn how to define, index, and iterate over tables so that you can store and get values on the fly. In addition, you will learn how to make functions that wrap up logic and run code in a modular way. We will learn how to use control structures and loops to manage the flow of our programs. We will also learn how to use built-in functions to change strings. Each topic will build on the one before it, getting you ready to write Lua programs that are more structured and dynamic.

Understanding Variables and Data Types

Exploring Lua's Dynamic Typing

In Lua, you can assign any type of value to a variable without declaring it first, which makes for a pretty flexible system. You'll get a chance to practice this by assigning a number to a variable and then changing it to a string without running into any errors.

Following is an example to get you started:

```
value = 100            -- value is a number
print("Number:", value)
value = "One Hundred"  -- now value is a string
print("String:", value)
```

In this example, you will see how the variable **value** first holds a numerical value and then a text value. Lua automatically handles these changes, freeing you from manual type management and allowing you to focus on the logic of our program.

Managing Variables and Assignments

You will learn that variables in Lua are created simply by assigning them a value. No explicit declaration is needed, and the same variable can store different data types throughout its lifecycle. This approach makes our code succinct and easier to maintain. We will practice assigning values to variables and printing them to verify that they hold the expected content.

For instance, you can write:

```
name = "Lua Enthusiast"
age = 30
isActive = true
unknown = nil
print("Name:", name)
print("Age:", age)
print("Active:", isActive)
print("Unknown:", unknown)
```

Here, you will observe that each variable holds a different data type: a string, a number, a boolean, and nil. We will understand that **nil** in Lua represents the absence of a useful value. This concept is of utmost importance when you want to check if a variable has been assigned any meaningful data or if it should trigger a default behavior in our scripts.

Differences Between Data Types

Each data type in Lua has its own characteristics and usage. We will examine these differences through practical examples. For numbers, you can perform arithmetic operations directly:

```
num1 = 10
num2 = 5
sum = num1 + num2
print("Sum of numbers:", sum)
```

This code demonstrates the simplicity of arithmetic in Lua. We will see that numbers can be added, subtracted, multiplied, or divided without any special syntax. In contrast, strings represent sequences of characters and can be concatenated using the concatenation operator (**..**):

```
firstName = "Lua"
lastName = "Developer"
fullName = firstName .. " " .. lastName
print("Full Name:", fullName)
```

You will learn how to merge text values to form meaningful messages. Booleans, which represent true or false values, are commonly used in conditional statements and logical operations. We will try out basic boolean logic:

```
isReady = true
isComplete = false
print("Is Ready:", isReady)
print("Is Complete:", isComplete)
```

Through these examples, you will recognize that booleans in Lua are straightforward and essential for decision-making processes in our code.

Experimenting with 'nil'

The concept of nil is unique in Lua as it signifies the absence of a value. We will understand that a variable can be explicitly set to nil, or it may be nil by default if it has not been assigned any value. This can be demonstrated as follows:

```
-- Initially, variable 'status' is nil because it hasn't been assigned.
print("Initial status:", status)
status = "Active"
print("Assigned status:", status)
status = nil
print("Reset status to nil:", status)
```

You'll see how nil is used to clear a variable's content or to check if a variable has been set. And you'll learn to use this behavior in situations where you need to verify the existence or absence of data.

Combining Data Types in Expressions

Lua is flexible, but you need to be aware of how it manages different types together. For arithmetic operations, Lua requires that operands be numbers. If you attempt to mix strings and numbers in arithmetic operations, Lua will raise an error.

For example, the following code will not work as expected:

```
-- This will produce an error because "100" is a string, not a number.
result = "100" + 50
```

```
print("Result:", result)
```

Instead, you must convert string representations of numbers to actual numbers using conversion functions if needed. Conversely, when concatenating strings, you use the concatenation operator. We can also convert numbers to strings for this purpose:

```
score = 85
message = "Your score is " .. tostring(score)
print(message)
```

This example teaches you that conversion functions like **tostring()** and **tonumber()** are essential when you want to combine or compare different data types reliably.

Sample Program: Play of Variables

For instance, you might create a script that takes user input and assigns it to a variable, then displays it back. Although Lua's standard interpreter does not have built-in functions for interactive input like some other languages, you can simulate this by predefining variables and manipulating them to see how data types interact.

Consider writing a script that calculates a simple arithmetic operation and then modifies one of the variables:

```
-- simple_calculation.lua
value = 20
multiplier = 2
result = value * multiplier
print("Initial result:", result)
-- Changing variable type by reassigning to a string
value = "Twenty"
print("Updated value:", value)
```

In this exercise, you will see firsthand how changing a variable's value from a number to a string affects subsequent operations. The Lua's flexibility in handling these transitions will become clear as you run the code and observe the outputs.

Experimenting with Implicit Type Conversion

Although Lua is dynamically typed, it does not perform implicit type conversion in operations that require matching data types. We will experiment with this concept by intentionally creating type mismatches to observe the error messages that Lua provides. This process will help you understand the importance of managing types explicitly when necessary.

For example:

```
-- Implicit conversion error demonstration
numValue = 10
strValue = "ten"
-- The following line will produce an error due to a type mismatch:
-- combined = numValue + strValue
-- print("Combined:", combined)
```

If you trigger these errors on purpose in our REPL sessions, you'll see how Lua handles problems with type mismatches. This gets you ready to write more solid code that handles different data types properly.

Tables as Arrays and Dictionaries

Using Tables as Arrays

You will start by using tables as arrays. In Lua, arrays are simply tables with sequential numeric keys. When you create an array, you typically define its elements in a list format.

For instance, consider the following script that stores a list of fruits:

```
fruits = {"apple", "banana", "cherry", "date"}
print("First fruit:", fruits[1])
print("Second fruit:", fruits[2])
print("Last fruit:", fruits[#fruits])
```

In this code, you assign a table to the variable **fruits** using curly braces, and Lua automatically assigns numeric keys starting at 1. The operator **#** gives you the length of the table, allowing you to access the last element. We will learn to iterate through the array using loops, such as the **for** loop, which can be written as:

```
for index = 1, #fruits do
```

```
    print("Fruit at position " .. index .. " is " ..
fruits[index])
end
```

By running this code, you will see how the table stores data sequentially, and you will experience how Lua handles array-like structures effectively.

Using Tables as Dictionaries

Next, you will explore tables as associative maps or dictionaries. In this usage, tables store data using keys that are not limited to sequential numbers. We can use strings, numbers, or even other data types as keys. This flexibility allows you to create mappings between unique identifiers and their associated values.

See the following example that uses a table to represent a person's profile:

```
person = {
    name = "Alex",
    age = 28,
    occupation = "Engineer"
}
print("Name:", person.name)
print("Age:", person.age)
print("Occupation:", person["occupation"])
```

Here in the above, you define a table with named keys, allowing you to access each element either by the dot notation or by square brackets with the key as a string. We will notice that this approach is particularly useful when you have data with clear identifiers, making our code more readable and organized.

Manipulating Tables

You will soon discover that tables are not static; you can add, modify, and remove elements dynamically. For instance, to add a new key-value pair to the **person** table, you can simply assign a new value:

```
person.email = "alex@example.com"
print("Email:", person.email)
```

If you wish to update an existing value, you can reassign it directly:

```
person.age = 29
print("Updated Age:", person.age)
```

Similarly, you can remove an element by assigning it to **nil**:

```
person.occupation = nil
```

After this operation, attempting to access **person.occupation** will return **nil**, indicating that the key no longer exists in the table. Through these exercises, you will learn how Lua's dynamic nature allows you to modify data structures in real time.

Iterating Over Tables

You will gain proficiency in iterating over tables, whether they serve as arrays or dictionaries. For arrays, you have already seen how a numeric **for** loop can be used. However, when dealing with dictionaries, the **pairs** function is our tool of choice. This function allows you to traverse all key-value pairs in a table without assuming any order:

```
for key, value in pairs(person) do
    print(key .. ":", value)
end
```

This loop will print each key and its corresponding value from the **person** table. Using **pairs** ensures that you can work with every element in the table, regardless of the key type. We will appreciate how this flexibility enables you to handle complex data structures with ease.

Nested Tables and Complex Structures

Tables can also be nested, allowing you to create more complex data structures. For instance, you might store a list of profiles within a single table:

```
people = {
    {name = "Alex", age = 28},
    {name = "Jordan", age = 32},
    {name = "Taylor", age = 25}
}
for index, individual in ipairs(people) do
```

```
    print("Profile " .. index .. ":")
    print("  Name: " .. individual.name)
    print("  Age: " .. individual.age)
end
```

In the above program, you create a table of tables where each inner table represents an individual's profile. We use the **ipairs** function to iterate over the array-like structure. As you work through nested tables, you will learn to navigate and manipulate multi-dimensional data, an essential skill for creating applications that manage complex datasets.

By working with tables as both arrays and dictionaries, you will be equipped to tackle a wide range of practical problems. Whether you are storing lists of items, mapping configurations, or organizing user data, tables provide the versatility needed for data storage and retrieval.

Function Definitions and Execution

Defining Functions

A function is declared using the keyword **function**, followed by its name and a parameter list enclosed in parentheses. Consider the following example:

```
-- Define a function that greets the user by name
function greet(name)
    return "Hello, " .. name .. "!"
end
-- Call the function and print its result
print(greet("Explorer"))
```

In the above, you define a function called **greet** that takes a single parameter, **name**. The function concatenates a greeting message with the provided name and returns the resulting string. When you invoke **greet** with the argument **"Explorer"**, the function returns **"Hello, Explorer!"**, which is a straightforward way to encapsulate behavior within a function.

Function Parameters and Return Values

You will notice that functions in Lua can accept multiple parameters and return values. Defining clear parameters helps you structure our code and makes it easier to reuse functions in different contexts.

For instance, you might create a function to calculate the area of a rectangle:

```
-- Define a function to calculate the area of a rectangle
function calculateArea(length, width)
    return length * width
end
-- Invoke the function with sample values
area = calculateArea(10, 5)
print("Area of rectangle:", area)
```

Here, **calculateArea** accepts two parameters, **length** and **width**, multiplies them, and returns the result. When you call the function with **10** and **5**, it computes the area as **50**. This reinforces how clear parameter definitions lead to predictable and reliable function behavior.

Functions as First-Class Values

One of the powerful aspects of Lua is that functions are first-class citizens. This means you can assign functions to variables, pass them as arguments to other functions, and even return them as values. We will experience this flexibility with the following example:

```
-- Assign a function to a variable
adder = function(a, b)
    return a + b
end
-- Use the function stored in the variable
result = adder(15, 25)
print("Result of addition:", result)
```

In the above, you assign an anonymous function that adds two numbers to the variable **adder**. We then call **adder** with arguments **15** and **25**, and the function returns **40**. This behavior highlights how functions can be manipulated like any other variable in Lua, offering a great deal of flexibility when designing our programs.

Passing Functions as Arguments

Lua allows you to pass functions as arguments to other functions. This capability is particularly useful when you need to abstract behavior or implement higher-order functions. Consider the following example:

```
-- Define a function that applies a given operation to two
numbers
function applyOperation(a, b, operation)
    return operation(a, b)
end
-- Define a couple of operations
function add(x, y)
    return x + y
end
function multiply(x, y)
    return x * y
end
-- Use the higher-order function with different operations
sum = applyOperation(8, 12, add)
product = applyOperation(8, 12, multiply)
print("Sum:", sum)
print("Product:", product)
```

In this example, you define a function called **applyOperation** that takes two numbers and a function **operation** as parameters. We then define two separate functions, **add** and **multiply**, and pass them as arguments to **applyOperation**. The higher-order function executes the passed operation on the given numbers, returning the result. This pattern demonstrates how passing functions as arguments can reduce redundancy by reusing function logic in different contexts.

Returning Functions from Functions

In addition to passing functions as arguments, you will also learn that functions can return other functions. This is particularly useful for creating closures or factory functions.

The following example illustrates this concept:

```
-- Define a function that returns another function
function makeGreeter(greeting)
    return function(name)
```

```
        return greeting .. ", " .. name .. "!"
    end
end
-- Create a specific greeter function and use it
sayHello = makeGreeter("Hello")
print(sayHello("Explorer"))
-- Create another greeter with a different greeting
sayHi = makeGreeter("Hi")
print(sayHi("Explorer"))
```

Here, **makeGreeter** is a function that takes a **greeting** string as an argument and returns a new function. The returned function, when called with a name, concatenates the greeting with the name. This shows how you can generate specialized functions on the fly based on provided parameters.

Sample Program: Role of Functions

Imagine you are building a simple calculator that can perform different operations based on user choice as shown below:

```
-- Simple Calculator using Functions
-- Define basic arithmetic functions
function add(x, y)
    return x + y
end
function subtract(x, y)
    return x - y
end
function multiply(x, y)
    return x * y
end
function divide(x, y)
    if y == 0 then
```

```
        return "Error: Division by zero"
    else
        return x / y
    end
end
-- Higher-order function to execute an operation
function calculate(a, b, operation)
    return operation(a, b)
end
-- Test the calculator functions
num1 = 20
num2 = 4
print("Addition:", calculate(num1, num2, add))
print("Subtraction:", calculate(num1, num2, subtract))
print("Multiplication:", calculate(num1, num2, multiply))
print("Division:", calculate(num1, num2, divide))
```

Here, you define several arithmetic functions for basic operations and a higher-order function **calculate** that takes two numbers and an operation. We are passing different arithmetic functions to **calculate**, through which you perform a variety of calculations. This concludes the idea of functions as first-class values and demonstrates how you can structure our code for maximum reuse and clarity.

Experimenting with Function Behavior

While practicing, you are encouraged to experiment by modifying function parameters, adding error handling, or extending functionality. For instance, you might try to create a function that accepts a variable number of arguments using the **...** syntax, which allows you to pass a flexible number of parameters:

```
-- Function to sum a variable number of arguments
function sumAll(...)
    local total = 0
    local numbers = {...}
```

```
    for i = 1, #numbers do
        total = total + numbers[i]
    end
    return total
end
print("Sum of numbers:", sumAll(1, 2, 3, 4, 5))
```

In the above program, **sumAll** uses the ellipsis (**...**) to collect all arguments into a table. The function then iterates over the table to compute the total sum. By playing around with these variations, you'll see how Lua's function features can do so much more, and you'll get a better idea of how functions work as flexible, reusable parts.

Control Structures and Looping Constructs

If-Statements for Decision-Making

You begin by learning how if- statements allow you to evaluate conditions and execute specific code based on the result. The basic syntax for an if- statement in Lua is straightforward:

```
number = 15
if number > 10 then
    print("The number is greater than 10.")
end
```

In this example, you compare a variable **number** with the value 10. When the condition evaluates to true, the code block following the if- statement is executed. We can also add an else branch to handle the opposite scenario:

```
if number > 20 then
    print("The number is greater than 20.")
else
    print("The number is not greater than 20.")
end
```

For more complex conditions, you may combine if- statements with elseif clauses to evaluate multiple conditions:

```
if number > 20 then
    print("The number is greater than 20.")
elseif number == 15 then
    print("The number is exactly 15.")
else
    print("The number is less than 15 and not greater than
20.")
end
```

Here, you will observe how Lua directs the program's flow based on our conditions.

While Loops for Repetition

Next, you will explore while loops, which allow you to repeat a block of code as long as a specified condition remains true. The while loop is useful when the number of iterations is not known in advance.

Let us try the following example:

```
counter = 1
while counter <= 5 do
    print("Counter is at:", counter)
    counter = counter + 1
end
```

Here in the above code, you initialize a counter variable and use a while loop to print its value until it exceeds 5. We will see how the loop continues to execute until the condition becomes false. Here, you got to know how the loop's behavior changes with different parameters.

For Loops for Iteration

For loops in Lua provide a concise way to iterate over a range of values or through elements in an array-like table. The numeric for loop is ideal when you know the number of iterations in advance. For example, you might write:

```
for i = 1, 5 do
    print("Iteration number:", i)
```

```
end
```

This loop sets the variable **i** to 1 and increases it by 1 after each iteration until it reaches 5. The loop executes the code block for each value of **i**, making it a reliable tool for repeating actions a fixed number of times.

When dealing with arrays or tables, you can also use the for loop in combination with the length operator. Suppose you have an array of names:

```
names = {"Alice", "Bob", "Charlie", "Dana"}
for index = 1, #names do
    print("Name at index " .. index .. " is " .. names[index])
end
```

This loop iterates over the table **names** by using the length operator (**#**) to determine the number of elements. We will observe how the loop accesses each element sequentially and prints it to the terminal.

Combining Control Structures

You can mix if-statements and loops to make more complex logic. For example, you might want to go through an array and do something specific for certain elements. Given below is an example to get you started:

```
numbers = {3, 7, 12, 5, 18, 9}
for index = 1, #numbers do
    if numbers[index] > 10 then
        print("Number " .. numbers[index] .. " is greater than 
10.")
    else
        print("Number " .. numbers[index] .. " is 10 or 
less.")
    end
end
```

Here, you iterate through the **numbers** table and use an if- statement within the for loop to check each number. This combination enables you to handle each element individually based on its value, ensuring that our code can adapt its behavior as it processes data.

Nested Loops for Multidimensional Data

In more advanced scenarios, you might encounter situations where nested loops are necessary to process multidimensional data. For example, if you have a table of tables representing a grid of values, you can use nested for loops to iterate over each row and column:

```
grid = {
    {1, 2, 3},
    {4, 5, 6},
    {7, 8, 9}
}
for row = 1, #grid do
    for col = 1, #grid[row] do
        print("Value at row " .. row .. ", col " .. col .. "
is " .. grid[row][col])
    end
end
```

In this example, the outer loop iterates over each row of the grid, while the inner loop iterates over each element within that row. All these control structures are going to be super important for our programming toolkit. They'll help you write more flexible and dynamic Lua scripts.

Utilizing String Manipulation

Basic String Functions

You begin by familiarizing yourself with some of Lua's most commonly used string functions. The **`string.upper`** and **`string.lower`** functions convert text to upper and lower case, respectively.

For instance, you can transform a message into all uppercase letters using the following code:

```
message = "Lua is fun and powerful."
upperMessage = string.upper(message)
print("Uppercase:", upperMessage)
```

Similarly, you can convert the same message to all lowercase letters:

```
lowerMessage = string.lower(message)
print("Lowercase:", lowerMessage)
```

These functions are useful when you need to standardize text data, such as ensuring that user input is processed in a consistent format. We also discover how to extract portions of a string with the **string.sub** function. In the code below, you extract a substring from the given text:

```
subMessage = string.sub(message, 5, 7)
print("Substring (characters 5 to 7):", subMessage)
```

This example shows how you can retrieve a specific segment of text by specifying the starting and ending positions. Such extraction is beneficial when you need to parse fixed-format data or isolate key components of a string.

Searching Patterns within Strings

Next, you learn how to search for specific patterns within a string using the **string.find** function. This function returns the starting and ending indices of the first occurrence of the specified pattern.

See the following example:

```
pattern = "fun"
startIndex, endIndex = string.find(message, pattern)
if startIndex then
    print("Pattern '" .. pattern .. "' found at position",
startIndex, "to", endIndex)
else
    print("Pattern '" .. pattern .. "' not found.")
end
```

In the above example, you search for the word "fun" in the message. The function returns the positions where the pattern is found, which you then print to the terminal. This technique is especially useful when you need to validate input or extract data based on recognizable markers within a text.

Apart form this, Lua's pattern matching capabilities extend beyond simple text search. We will encounter special characters and character classes that let you match digits, letters, or even whitespace. Let us think of s situation wherein we want to find a sequence of digits within a string. For this, we might use:

```
textWithNumbers = "The year is 2025."
numberStart, numberEnd = string.find(textWithNumbers, "%d+")
if numberStart then
    print("Number found:", string.sub(textWithNumbers,
numberStart, numberEnd))
end
```

Here, **%d+** represents one or more digits, and Lua returns the location of this sequence. We will appreciate the powerful pattern matching Lua does in order to process and validate complex text data.

Replacing and Transforming Text

Another critical aspect of string manipulation is replacing parts of a string using the **string.gsub** function. This function searches for a pattern and replaces all occurrences with a specified replacement string.

In the sample program below, you replace every occurrence of the word "Lua" with "Awesome Lua":

```
newMessage, replacements = string.gsub(message, "Lua",
"Awesome Lua")
print("After replacement:", newMessage)
print("Number of replacements:", replacements)
```

The function returns the modified string along with the count of replacements made. This capability is particularly useful when you need to sanitize or format text, such as correcting user input or generating customized messages.

Additionally, you can use **string.format** to create formatted strings that combine variables with fixed text. For example:

```
name = "Explorer"
score = 95
formattedString = string.format("Congratulations %s, our score
is %d.", name, score)
print(formattedString)
```

This formatted output is similar to what you might find in other programming languages, and it provides a neat way to build strings that include variable content in a controlled format.

Sample Program: Combining String Manipulation Techniques

Let us work through a comprehensive sample program that combines various string manipulation techniques. This program processes a sentence by converting its case, extracting substrings, searching for specific words, and replacing certain text elements.

Consider the following program:

```
-- Sample program for string manipulation in Lua
-- Original text message
originalText = "Lua is fun, dynamic, and powerful. Learning
Lua opens many doors."
-- Convert to uppercase and lowercase
upperText = string.upper(originalText)
lowerText = string.lower(originalText)
print("Original:", originalText)
print("Uppercase:", upperText)
print("Lowercase:", lowerText)
-- Extract a substring: extract the first sentence
periodPosition = string.find(originalText, "%.")
if periodPosition then
    firstSentence = string.sub(originalText, 1,
periodPosition)
    print("First sentence:", firstSentence)
end
-- Search for a pattern: find the word "dynamic"
searchPattern = "dynamic"
startPos, endPos = string.find(originalText, searchPattern)
if startPos then
    print("The word '" .. searchPattern .. "' found from
position", startPos, "to", endPos)
else
```

```
    print("The word '" .. searchPattern .. "' was not found.")
end
-- Replace the word "Lua" with "Lua Programming"
modifiedText, count = string.gsub(originalText, "Lua", "Lua Programming")
print("Modified text:", modifiedText)
print("Replacements made:", count)
-- Create a formatted string combining variables
name = "Explorer"
activity = "coding"
formattedOutput = string.format("Hello %s, welcome to %s in Lua!", name, activity)
print(formattedOutput)
```

Here, you observe how multiple string functions come together to manipulate text. We convert the case of a sentence, extract a segment based on punctuation, search for a keyword, and perform global replacements. The program also demonstrates how to combine variable content with fixed text using formatting. We run the code in our Lua interpreter and see immediate feedback, which reinforces our understanding of how these string manipulation techniques work.

Summary

Overall, you learned a lot about Lua's basic building blocks and gained a deep understanding of its data structures and programming blocks. We began by learning about variables and data types. This is where you discovered that Lua's dynamic typing let you assign values on the fly without making explicit declarations. We learned about how numbers, strings, booleans, and nil were used to store information and tried out these types by writing code examples.

Next, you moved on to using tables and learned that they could be used as both arrays and associative maps, which made it easier to store, retrieve, and change data. We learned how to access elements, add and change key-value pairs, and move through tables using different loop techniques through iterative exercises. We also learned how to define and run functions and understood that functions were normal objects that could be stored in variables, passed as parameters, and returned by other functions.

As you learned how to use if statements, while loops, and for loops to control the flow of our programs, control structures became very important. The last thing you did was manipulate strings by using built-in functions to change text, extract substrings, and search for patterns effectively.

All of these exercises gave you a solid background in Lua programming and the skills you need to move on to more difficult problems in later chapters.

CHAPTER 3: FILE I/O AND SCRIPTING TECHNIQUES

Overview

The practical side of using Lua to work with files and scripts is covered in this chapter. To start, you will learn how to open, read, write, and close files on a Linux system. We will learn how to use Lua's built-in functions to work with external data sources and efficiently handle file operations. Doing these tasks will help you build the skills you need to store, retrieve, and change data directly from files, which will prepare you for more advanced data processing.

The next part is data parsing and manipulation, where you will learn how to get text data from files and change it. We will learn how to find and fix errors that happen when you work with files in this chapter. This will make sure that our scripts can handle problems that come up quickly. Lastly, you will learn how to include Lua scripts in larger programs, which will let you add more features and automatically do tasks on the fly. These topics will help you learn how to use Lua to make strong, data-driven apps.

File Handling Basics

Opening Files

Lua provides a simple way to open files using the built-in **io.open** function. We will learn that this function requires a file name and a mode, such as read, write, or append. For example, to open a file for reading, you can use the following code:

```
file = io.open("example.txt", "r")
if file then
    print("File opened successfully for reading.")
else
    print("Failed to open file.")
end
```

In this code, you attempt to open "example.txt" in read mode. The function returns a file handle if the file is found and opened; otherwise, it returns nil.

Reading from Files

Once a file is open, you can read its contents using methods provided by the file handle. Lua offers several functions such as **:read("*all")** to read the entire file or **:read("*line")** to read one line at a time. The following example demonstrates how to read the entire content of a file:

```
file = io.open("example.txt", "r")
if file then
    content = file:read("*all")
    print("File content:")
    print(content)
    file:close()
else
    print("Error: Unable to read the file.")
end
```

Here, you open the file in read mode, then use **:read("*all")** to capture all the text. After printing the content, you close the file.

Writing to Files

Writing data to files is another critical operation that you will master using Lua's file I/O libraries. To write to a file, you typically open it in write mode ("w") or append mode ("a"). In write mode, the file is created if it does not exist, and its content is overwritten if it already exists.

Given below is an example that writes a simple message to a file:

```
file = io.open("output.txt", "w")
if file then
    file:write("Hello, Lua! This is a test message written to
the file.\n")
    file:write("File writing in Lua is simple and
effective.\n")
    print("Data written successfully to output.txt.")
    file:close()
else
    print("Error: Unable to open file for writing.")
end
```

This above program opens "output.txt" in write mode, writes two lines of text to it, and then closes the file. We will witness that closing the file is so crucial to ensure that all data is saved properly and resources are freed.

Appending Data

Appending data to an existing file without overwriting its contents is done by opening the file in append mode ("a"). We will see how this mode is useful for logging or gradually adding data to a file.

See the following example:

```
file = io.open("output.txt", "a")
if file then
    file:write("Appending a new line to the file.\n")
    print("Data appended successfully to output.txt.")
    file:close()
else
    print("Error: Unable to open file for appending.")
end
```

Here, you open the same file in append mode and add an extra line of text. This approach is particularly useful when you want to maintain a history of events or continuously update a file without losing previous information.

Handling File Errors

While performing file I/O, you may encounter situations where a file cannot be opened or read. Lua's file handling functions return nil when an error occurs, allowing you to implement error checking. We will learn to incorporate conditional statements to handle such cases gracefully.

Let us consider the following approach to safely open and read a file:

```
file, err = io.open("nonexistent.txt", "r")
if not file then
    print("Error opening file:", err)
else
    content = file:read("*all")
    print("Content of file:")
    print(content)
    file:close()
```

```
end
```

In this code, if the file "nonexistent.txt" does not exist, **`io.open`** returns nil and an error message, which you then print. This practice helps you design robust scripts that can manage file I/O errors without crashing.

Throughout our work with file I/O, you will develop several best practices that enhance the reliability and efficiency of our code. Always check the return value of **`io.open`** before proceeding with any file operations. Ensure that you use appropriate file modes depending on whether you intend to read, write, or append data. And you must also close every file after completing operations to maintain system stability and data integrity. This whole foundation in file handling is very much of use once you move on to more complex scripting techniques and larger projects.

Data Parsing and Manipulation

Sample CSV File Overview

Imagine you have a CSV file named "data.csv" with the following contents:

csv

```
name,age,score

Alice,30,88.5

Bob,25,92

Charlie,35,78.2
```

This file contains three columns: name, age, and score. Your goal is to read this file, parse each line into separate values, convert numeric values from strings to numbers, and store the data in a Lua table for further analysis. This transformation allows you to perform operations such as calculating averages, filtering records, or summarizing data.

Reading the CSV File

You start by opening the CSV file in read mode and then reading its entire content. The code below demonstrates how to open "data.csv", read all lines, and then close the file:

```
-- Open the CSV file in read mode

local file = io.open("data.csv", "r")

if not file then
```

```
    error("Failed to open file 'data.csv'.")
end
-- Read all lines from the file
local fileContent = file:read("*all")
file:close()
-- Print the file content (for debugging purposes)
print("File Content:\n" .. fileContent)
```

Here, you ensure that the file is successfully opened before reading its content. The entire file is stored in the variable **`fileContent`**, which will later be processed line by line.

Splitting File Content into Lines

Next, you need to split the file content into individual lines. This is done by iterating over each line using Lua's pattern matching. We create an empty table to store the lines and then use a pattern that matches each line ending with a newline character:

```
local lines = {}
for line in fileContent:gmatch("[^\r\n]+") do
    table.insert(lines, line)
end
-- Print the number of lines read
print("Total lines read:", #lines)
```

Here, the pattern **`[^\r\n]+`** matches sequences of characters that are not newline characters. This loop populates the **`lines`** table with each row from the CSV file, including the header row.

Parsing Each Line into Fields

Now that you have the file split into lines, you will parse each line to extract the individual fields. Since the data is comma-separated, you can use Lua's pattern matching to split each line on commas. We will process the header separately to identify column names and then parse the remaining lines into a structured format:

```
-- Function to split a string by a given delimiter
local function split(input, delimiter)
    local result = {}
```

```
    for match in (input .. delimiter):gmatch("(.-)" ..
delimiter) do
        table.insert(result, match)
    end
    return result
end
-- Extract header fields
local header = split(lines[1], ",")
print("Header fields:")
for i, field in ipairs(header) do
    print(field)
end
-- Parse data lines into a table of records
local data = {}
for i = 2, #lines do
    local fields = split(lines[i], ",")
    local record = {}
    for j, key in ipairs(header) do
        record[key] = fields[j]
    end
    table.insert(data, record)
end
-- Print the parsed records
print("Parsed Records:")
for i, record in ipairs(data) do
    print("Record " .. i .. ":")
    for key, value in pairs(record) do
        print("  " .. key .. ":", value)
    end
```

```
end
```

In this code, the **split** function is defined to divide a string into parts based on the provided delimiter. We first split the header line to get column names, then iterate over each subsequent line, splitting it into fields and creating a record (a Lua table) that maps header keys to their corresponding values. Each record is added to the **data** table.

Converting Data Types

The data read from the file is stored as strings, but some fields, such as age and score, should be treated as numbers for analysis. We will now loop through each record and convert these fields to numeric values where applicable:

```
for i, record in ipairs(data) do
    -- Convert age and score to numbers
    record.age = tonumber(record.age)
    record.score = tonumber(record.score)
end
-- Verify conversion by printing records again
print("Records After Type Conversion:")
for i, record in ipairs(data) do
    print("Record " .. i .. ":")
    for key, value in pairs(record) do
        print("  " .. key .. ":", value, "(" .. type(value) ..
")")
    end
end
```

Here, the **tonumber** function is used to convert the strings representing age and score into numbers. This is another important step for any subsequent numerical calculations or comparisons.

Analyzing Data

With the data now structured and converted to the proper types, you can perform analysis on it. As an example, you might calculate the average score of the records as shown below:

```
local totalScore = 0
local count = 0
for i, record in ipairs(data) do
    if record.score then
        totalScore = totalScore + record.score
        count = count + 1
    end
end
if count > 0 then
    local averageScore = totalScore / count
    print("Average Score:", averageScore)
else
    print("No valid scores to compute average.")
end
```

This code iterates through the **data** table, summing the scores and counting the records. The average score is then calculated by dividing the total score by the count of valid records, which tells us how we can use parsed data to derive meaningful insights.

Advanced Data Transformation

Beyond basic parsing and conversion, you might need to transform the data further. For instance, you could filter records based on certain criteria. Suppose you want to extract records where the score is above a specific threshold:

```
local highScorers = {}
local threshold = 90
for i, record in ipairs(data) do
    if record.score and record.score > threshold then
        table.insert(highScorers, record)
    end
end
print("High Scorers (Score > " .. threshold .. "):")
```

```
for i, record in ipairs(highScorers) do
    print("Name: " .. record.name .. ", Score: " ..
record.score)
end
```

This snippet creates a new table **highScorers** and populates it with records that meet the condition of having a score greater than 90. By applying such filters, you can tailor the dataset to specific analysis needs.

Error Handling in File Operations

Checking File Existence and Handling Open Failures

One of the most common errors in file I/O is failing to open a file. We will learn to check if a file exists and is accessible by inspecting the return value of the **io.open** function.

For example, consider the following code:

```
local file, err = io.open("data.csv", "r")
if not file then
    print("Error opening file 'data.csv':", err)
    -- Implement fallback: provide a default value or log the
error
    -- You might exit the function or return from the script
safely
    return
end
```

Here, the function returns both a file handle and an error message if the file cannot be opened. If the file is nil, you can print the error message and take necessary fallback actions. This approach prevents our script from continuing with invalid file operations and causing further issues.

Using Protected Calls for Safe File Operations

Lua provides the **pcall** (protected call) function to execute code that may cause runtime errors without halting the entire program. We can wrap file operations in a protected call to catch errors.

For instance:

```
local success, content = pcall(function()
    local f = io.open("data.csv", "r")
    if not f then error("File not found") end
    local data = f:read("*all")
    f:close()
    return data
end)
if success then
    print("File content successfully read.")
    print(content)
else
    print("An error occurred during file operations:",
content)
    -- Fallback strategy: Use a backup file or prompt the user
to check the file
end
```

Here, you encapsulate the file reading operations inside a function passed to **pcall**. If any error occurs, the error message is captured and you can decide how to handle it without crashing our script.

Implementing Fallback Strategies

When an error occurs, it is important to have a fallback strategy that prevents data loss or application failure. We might choose to use a default file, log the error for further review, or provide an alternative operation.

Consider the following example:

```
local file, err = io.open("data.csv", "r")
if not file then
    print("Warning: Could not open 'data.csv'. Using default
data instead.")
    -- Fallback: Provide a default CSV string
    defaultData = "name,age,score\nDefault,0,0"
```

```
    fileContent = defaultData
else
    fileContent = file:read("*all")
    file:close()
end
print("Processed Data:")
print(fileContent)
```

In this code, if "data.csv" cannot be opened, you print a warning and assign a default CSV string to continue processing. This approach ensures that our application can operate even when the expected file is missing.

Handling Write Errors and Data Integrity

When you're writing data to a file, it's as important to check if it's open and closed properly because if something goes wrong during writing, you might lose our data.

For example:

```
local file, err = io.open("output.txt", "w")
if not file then
    print("Error: Unable to open 'output.txt' for writing:",
err)
    -- Fallback: You may decide to write to a temporary file
instead
    return
end
local status, errMsg = pcall(function()
    file:write("Hello, Lua! This is a safe write
operation.\n")
end)
if not status then
    print("Error writing to file:", errMsg)
    -- Optionally, handle partial writes or attempt to save to
an alternative file
```

```
end
local closeStatus, closeErr = pcall(function()
    file:close()
end)
if not closeStatus then
    print("Error closing the file:", closeErr)
    -- Fallback: Handle cleanup as needed
end
```

In the above, you check for errors during the file open, write, and close stages. Using **pcall** helps catch any runtime issues, and you implement fallback messages so that you know exactly what went wrong.

Logging Errors for Debugging

In addition to providing fallbacks, you might want to log errors to a file for debugging purposes. Creating an error log helps you track recurring issues and understand what may be causing problems in our file operations.

For example:

```
local function logError(message)
    local logFile, err = io.open("error.log", "a")
    if logFile then
        logFile:write(os.date("%Y-%m-%d %H:%M:%S") .. " - " ..
message .. "\n")
        logFile:close()
    else
        print("Error: Unable to open log file:", err)
    end
end
local file, err = io.open("data.csv", "r")
if not file then
    local errorMsg = "Failed to open data.csv: " .. err
```

```
    print(errorMsg)
    logError(errorMsg)
    return
end
```

This code defines a **logError** function that writes error messages to "error.log" with a timestamp. When a file operation doesn't work, you should record the error before trying other solutions. This helps with immediate debugging and long-term maintenance by keeping a record of issues.

Testing Error Handling

When you're working on error handling strategies, it's important to test our script in different situations to make sure it's working right. One thing you can do is rename a file to act like it's missing, or change the file permissions to show access problems. These tests will help you see if our backup plans are good and if our script can handle things when they go wrong.

For example, you can temporarily set up a scenario where the file does not exist:

```
local file, err = io.open("nonexistent.csv", "r")
if not file then
    local errorMsg = "nonexistent.csv does not exist: " .. err
    print(errorMsg)
    logError(errorMsg)
    -- Fallback: Use default data
    defaultData = "name,age,score\nDefault,0,0"
    fileContent = defaultData
else
    fileContent = file:read("*all")
    file:close()
end
print("Final Data Processed:")
print(fileContent)
```

In this test, the script attempts to open a non-existent file and then falls back to default data while logging the error. Such validates that our script remains functional in adverse conditions. With all these examples, you learned how to handle any errors that could pop up during our file operations.

Embedding Lua Scripts

Methods for Integrating Lua Scripts

You have multiple options for embedding Lua scripts. The simplest method is using **dofile** to execute an external Lua file. This method allows you to load and run a script as part of our main application. Alternatively, you can use **require** to load modules that return tables or functions. In more advanced scenarios, you might embed Lua in a host application written in C or another language using Lua's C API, which offers greater control over the integration process.

Let us think of an example wherein the main Lua application needs to call an embedded script to perform a specific task. So here, you might structure our code as follows:

```
-- main.lua: Main application file
print("Main Application Starting...")
-- Load and execute the embedded Lua script
local status, err = pcall(function()
    dofile("embedded_script.lua")
end)
if not status then
    print("Error during script integration:", err)
    -- Implement fallback: log the error or continue with
default behavior
else
    print("Embedded script executed successfully.")
end
print("Main Application Continues...")
```

In this sample, you use **pcall** to catch any errors that occur during the execution of **embedded_script.lua**. This helps prevent the entire application from crashing if the embedded script fails.

Common Integration Errors

While integrating Lua scripts, you may encounter several common errors. It is important to understand these errors and implement strategies to overcome them.

Error 1: File Not Found

One frequent issue is attempting to load a file that does not exist. For example, if **embedded_script.lua** is missing or its path is incorrect, **dofile** will throw an error. To handle this, you check the file's existence before attempting to load it, or you catch the error with **pcall**:

```
local function loadScript(filename)
    local file = io.open(filename, "r")
    if not file then
        error("File '" .. filename .. "' not found.")
    else
        file:close()
        dofile(filename)
    end
end
local status, err = pcall(loadScript, "embedded_script.lua")
if not status then
    print("File not found error handled:", err)
    -- Fallback: Execute default script or use built-in
functionality
end
```

This approach ensures that if the file is not present, you log the error and fall back gracefully.

Error 2: Syntax Errors in the Embedded Script

If the embedded Lua script contains a syntax error, executing it with **dofile** will cause an error. To manage this, you again use **pcall** to catch the syntax error and provide useful feedback:

```
local status, err = pcall(function()
    dofile("embedded_script_with_syntax_error.lua")
end)
if not status then
```

```
    print("Syntax error in embedded script:", err)
    -- Fallback: Alert the developer or load a corrected
version of the script
end
```

If you catch syntax errors, you can stop the error from spreading and crashing the main application. This lets you debug and fix the embedded script without messing up the overall functionality.

Error 3: Runtime Errors in the Embedded Script

Sometimes the embedded script may run into runtime errors—such as division by zero or nil value access—that were not caught during the load time. Using **pcall** helps capture these runtime issues as well:

```
local status, err = pcall(function()
    dofile("embedded_script_with_runtime_error.lua")
end)
if not status then
    print("Runtime error occurred during script execution:",
err)
    -- Fallback: Switch to a safe mode or use default data
end
```

This method ensures that even if the embedded script fails during execution, the error is caught, and our main application continues to run. Additionally, you can log these errors for later debugging.

Best Practices for Safe Integration

To ensure a smooth integration of Lua scripts into our application, consider the following practices:

- Always wrap script execution in **pcall** or similar mechanisms to catch errors.
- Validate file existence and paths before loading scripts.
- Use logging functions to record errors with detailed messages and timestamps.
- Design fallback strategies, such as default configurations or alternative workflows, to maintain application stability.

- When embedding scripts from external sources, sanitize input and verify that the script content meets security standards.

If you make these practices a part of our process, then you've got a solid system in place where you can update or replace Lua scripts without messing with the main application's stability. Plus, you'll learn how to handle any hiccups that might pop up, making sure that errors are taken care of smoothly and that the application stays reliable in different situations.

Summary

In conclusion, you learned how to use Lua to work with files and scripts in a very thorough way. We learned how to manage persistent data storage by working with real code examples while exploring Lua's file I/O libraries. We saw how to read data from a CSV file, split it up into lines, and then turn each line into a record that makes sense. For more in-depth analysis, you were also taught how to change raw string data into formats that can be used.

Then, you looked at different ways to handle errors and catch exceptions that happened while working with files. We learned how to record errors, which helped you fix problems and keep the data safe. We also practiced using dofile and require to add Lua scripts to bigger programs, and you learned how to fix common integration problems like missing files, syntax errors, and runtime errors. The hands-on activities taught you how to make strong, modular programs that could safely connect to outside data sources and handle mistakes with grace.

CHAPTER 4: ADVANCED PROGRAMMING CONSTRUCTS

Overview

This chapter will teach you more advanced programming concepts that will help you understand how Lua works better. We will learn to use metatables and operator overloading to change how tables behave and add to the language's features. This will make our data structures more flexible and expressive. We will additionally find out about concurrency coroutines to handle multiple tasks without using traditional multithreading. By trying these methods out, you will learn how to manage the flow of programs and make them work well, without any problems, and able to smoothly handle complicated tasks.

Within this chapter, you will discover more about advanced function techniques and closures, which let you hide state and create modular, reusable code. And finally, you will learn to debug advanced Lua constructs, which will help you find and fix complex problems quickly. Collectively, these topics will give you a strong set of skills to handle difficult programming tasks and create fast, scalable Lua apps.

Metatables and Operator Overloading

In this section, you will explore metatables. It is a powerful Lua feature that allows you to customize the behavior of tables. Metatables are special tables that can define how a table reacts to various operations such as addition, subtraction, or even function calls. Through operator overloading, you can override Lua's default behavior for operators, enabling you to implement customized interactions between tables and external operations.

Metatables also allow you to attach a separate table to an existing table, which can define behaviors for common operations. When you perform an operation on a table, Lua checks if the table has a metatable with a corresponding metamethod (special function). For example, the metamethod **__add** can be defined to customize what happens when two tables are added using the **+** operator. With metatables, you can extend or modify default behaviors without changing the original table structure. We will learn to set a metatable for a table and how to define metamethods that override operations such as addition.

Setting up Metatable

To begin using metatables, you first create a table that will serve as our metatable and then assign it to another table using the **setmetatable** function. Consider a simple example where you define a metatable to override the behavior of the addition operator. In this case, you will create a table that represents a complex number with real and imaginary parts and then define how two complex numbers should be added.

```
-- Define a table representing a complex number
local complex1 = { real = 3, imag = 4 }
```

```
local complex2 = { real = 1, imag = 2 }
-- Create a metatable for operator overloading
local complexMeta = {}
-- Define the __add metamethod to overload the '+' operator
complexMeta.__add = function(a, b)
    -- a and b are tables representing complex numbers
    return {
        real = a.real + b.real,
        imag = a.imag + b.imag
    }
end
-- Attach the metatable to both complex numbers
setmetatable(complex1, complexMeta)
setmetatable(complex2, complexMeta)
```

In the above, you defined two complex number tables and a metatable called **`complexMeta`**. The metamethod **`__add`** is implemented as a function that takes two complex numbers (tables) and returns a new complex number by adding their respective real and imaginary parts. By using **`setmetatable`**, you assign this metatable to our complex number tables so that Lua uses our custom **`__add`** function when you use the **`+`** operator.

Customizing Other Operations

In addition to the addition operator, you can override many other operators and behaviors using metatables. For example, you might want to overload the subtraction operator (**`__sub`**) or the multiplication operator (**`__mul`**).

Below is an example that extends our complex number implementation to include subtraction:

```
-- Define the __sub metamethod to overload the '-' operator
complexMeta.__sub = function(a, b)
    return {
        real = a.real - b.real,
        imag = a.imag - b.imag
```

```
    }
end
-- Test the subtraction operator
local resultSub = complex1 - complex2
print("Result of subtraction:")
print("Real part:", resultSub.real)
print("Imaginary part:", resultSub.imag)
```

By adding a new metamethod **__sub**, you enable Lua to handle subtraction between tables with our custom logic. We can define similar metamethods for other operators like multiplication (**__mul**), division (**__div**), or even more complex operations such as indexing (**__index**) and new indexing (**__newindex**).

'__index' and '__newindex' Metamethods

Metatables also allow you to customize table indexing behaviors. The **__index** metamethod is called when you try to access a key that does not exist in a table. This is useful for implementing default values or inheritance-like features.

```
-- Create a prototype table with default properties
local defaults = { color = "red", size = "medium" }
-- Define a table for an object without explicit properties
local item = {}
-- Set a metatable for 'item' with an __index metamethod
setmetatable(item, { __index = defaults })
-- Accessing a non-existent key in 'item' will return the
default from 'defaults'
print("Item color:", item.color)  -- Output: red
print("Item size:", item.size)    -- Output: medium
```

In the above example, if a key is missing from **item**, Lua automatically looks up that key in the **defaults** table. We can also define the **__newindex** metamethod to control the behavior when assigning values to keys that do not exist, providing further customization over how our table behaves.

When using metatables and operator overloading, it is important to follow some best practices.

Ensure that our metamethods are clearly defined and that the returned values maintain a consistent structure. Avoid modifying metatables dynamically during critical operations, as this may lead to unpredictable behavior. Use clear naming conventions and document our custom behavior so that other developers (or our future self) can understand the intended functionality.

Debugging Metatable Behavior

While metatables provide great flexibility, they can also introduce complexity that makes debugging challenging. If our operator overloading does not work as expected, verify that the metatable is correctly attached to all relevant tables. We can print the metatable of a table using **getmetatable** to ensure it has the right properties:

```
local mt = getmetatable(complex1)
if mt then
    print("Metatable is set for complex1.")
else
    print("No metatable found for complex1.")
end
```

Also, be sure to include error checks in our metamethods. For example, when overloading operators, you'll want to make sure both operands are tables with the right structure. Adding conditional checks and error messages will help you spot issues early on.

When you integrate metatables into our Lua programming, you'll enhance our ability to define customized behaviors for tables. You'll learn to override default operations like addition and subtraction and to use metamethods for indexing. With all these examples and tips, you've got the skills to make our Lua code more robust, modular, and object-like. This feature of Lua not only simplifies complex operations, but it also opens up new possibilities for code abstraction and reuse in our projects.

Coroutines for Concurrency

Coroutines allow you to suspend and resume functions at specific points in their execution, making it possible to manage concurrent tasks without the overhead of operating system threads. Coroutines in Lua are similar to functions but can pause execution using the **coroutine.yield** function and then resume later using **coroutine.resume**. This behavior allows you to implement non-blocking operations in a cooperative manner. Unlike preemptive multitasking, where the operating system manages context switching, coroutines give you full control over when a task pauses and resumes, making it easier to debug and reason about our code. We will see how coroutines enable you to perform long-running operations, such as processing large datasets or waiting for I/O events, without freezing the main program flow.

Creating and Running Coroutines

We will now create a coroutine using the **coroutine.create** function, which wraps a function to become a coroutine. The coroutine does not start executing immediately; instead, you initiate it with **coroutine.resume**.

For example, consider the following program:

```
-- Define a coroutine function
local function worker()
    print("Coroutine started.")
    for i = 1, 3 do
        print("Processing step", i)
        coroutine.yield()  -- Pause execution after each step
    end
    print("Coroutine finished.")
end
-- Create a coroutine from the function
local co = coroutine.create(worker)
-- Resume the coroutine multiple times to see its behavior
print("Main program resumes coroutine:")
coroutine.resume(co)  -- Starts and runs until the first yield
coroutine.resume(co)  -- Resumes from the previous yield
coroutine.resume(co)  -- Continues execution
coroutine.resume(co)  -- Completes the coroutine execution
```

In this example, you define a **worker** function that simulates a task by iterating through a loop and yielding after each iteration. The **coroutine.create** function converts **worker** into a coroutine. Using **coroutine.resume**, you control the execution of the coroutine step by step. Each call to **coroutine.resume** restarts execution from where it was last paused, allowing you to interleave coroutine execution with other tasks in the main program.

Managing Concurrent Tasks

You can use coroutines to handle multiple tasks at the same time. If you create a bunch of coroutines and then run them in a round-robin fashion, you can make it seem like they're running at the same time.

Given below is an example of a program where two coroutines do different things:

```
-- Define two coroutine functions
local function task1()
    for i = 1, 5 do
        print("Task 1, iteration", i)
        coroutine.yield()
    end
end
local function task2()
    for i = 1, 5 do
        print("Task 2, iteration", i)
        coroutine.yield()
    end
end
-- Create coroutines for each task
local co1 = coroutine.create(task1)
local co2 = coroutine.create(task2)
-- Schedule the coroutines in a round-robin manner
local tasks = { co1, co2 }
local active = true
while active do
    active = false
    for _, co in ipairs(tasks) do
        if coroutine.status(co) ~= "dead" then
            coroutine.resume(co)
            active = true
        end
```

```
    end
end
print("All tasks completed.")
```

In this program, you create two tasks and place them in a table. A loop iterates over the table, resuming each coroutine in turn. The loop continues until all coroutines have completed their execution (i.e., their status becomes "dead"). This scheduling strategy demonstrates how you can simulate concurrent operations without complex thread management.

While coroutines are powerful, you need to be mindful of their cooperative nature. Since coroutines yield control explicitly, long-running operations within a coroutine that do not yield will block other tasks. Therefore, you should design our coroutine functions to yield frequently, especially when performing time-consuming computations.

Advanced Function Techniques and Closures

Closures and State Encapsulation

Closures in Lua are functions that capture variables from their surrounding environment. When a function is defined inside another function, the inner function retains access to the outer function's local variables even after the outer function has finished executing. This property allows you to encapsulate state, effectively creating private variables that are not accessible from the global scope.

For example, you can create a counter function that maintains its own state:

```
-- Define a function that returns a counter closure
function createCounter()
    local count = 0  -- 'count' is encapsulated within the
closure
    return function()
        count = count + 1
        return count
    end
end
-- Create a new counter instance and use it
local counter1 = createCounter()
```

```
print("Counter1:", counter1())  -- Output: 1
print("Counter1:", counter1())  -- Output: 2
-- Create a separate counter instance
local counter2 = createCounter()
print("Counter2:", counter2())  -- Output: 1
```

In this example, each call to **createCounter** produces a new function that holds its own **count** variable. The inner function can access and update this state, demonstrating how closures facilitate encapsulation.

Higher-Order Functions

Lua treats functions as first- class citizens, meaning you can pass functions as parameters, return them from other functions, or store them in variables. This ability allows you to build higher- order functions that operate on other functions. A common pattern is to create a function that modifies the behavior of another function.

For instance, you might write a function that logs the arguments and result of another function:

```
-- Define a higher-order function for logging
function withLogging(func)
    return function(...)
        local args = {...}
        print("Calling function with arguments:", 
table.concat(args, ", "))
        local result = func(...)
        print("Function returned:", result)
        return result
    end
end
-- Define a simple function to add two numbers
function add(a, b)
    return a + b
end
-- Wrap the 'add' function with logging
```

```
local loggedAdd = withLogging(add)
loggedAdd(10, 20)  -- Logs the call and the result
```

In this example, the **withLogging** function takes any function **func** and returns a new function that logs its arguments and result before returning the original result. This illustrates how higher- order functions can add behavior to existing functions without modifying them directly.

Creating Modular, Reusable Code Blocks

If you combine closures and higher-order functions, you can build highly modular code that's reusable and easy to maintain. For example, say you need to create customized greeting functions based on different greeting messages. Using closures, you can generate such functions dynamically.

```
-- Define a function that returns a custom greeter function
function createGreeter(greeting)
    return function(name)
        return greeting .. ", " .. name .. "!"
    end
end
-- Create two different greeter functions
local sayHello = createGreeter("Hello")
local sayHi = createGreeter("Hi")
print(sayHello("Explorer"))  -- Output: Hello, Explorer!
print(sayHi("Explorer"))     -- Output: Hi, Explorer!
```

Here, the **createGreeter** function encapsulates the greeting message within the returned closure, enabling you to generate multiple customized functions that share common logic but maintain separate state.

Sample Program: Task Scheduler

To illustrate advanced function techniques and closures in a more comprehensive scenario, consider a simple task scheduler. The scheduler will allow you to register tasks, each encapsulated within a closure that maintains its own state, and then execute them sequentially. This example highlights the use of closures for state encapsulation and higher- order functions for managing tasks.

```
-- Define a task scheduler that stores tasks in a table
local TaskScheduler = {}
-- Create a new scheduler instance
function TaskScheduler:new()
    local scheduler = { tasks = {} }
    setmetatable(scheduler, self)
    self.__index = self
    return scheduler
end
-- Add a task to the scheduler; each task is a function
function TaskScheduler:addTask(taskFunc)
    table.insert(self.tasks, taskFunc)
end
-- Run all tasks sequentially
function TaskScheduler:runTasks()
    for index, task in ipairs(self.tasks) do
        print("Running Task " .. index .. ":")
        task()  -- Execute the task, which may be a closure
with its own state
    end
end
-- Create a scheduler instance
local scheduler = TaskScheduler:new()
-- Add a task that counts from 1 to 3
scheduler:addTask(function()
    local count = 0
    for i = 1, 3 do
        count = count + 1
        print("Task 1 count:", count)
```

```
        -- Simulate some work with a yield or pause if needed
    end
end)
-- Add a task that greets multiple names using a closure
scheduler:addTask(function()
    local greeter = createGreeter("Greetings")
    local names = { "Alice", "Bob", "Charlie" }
    for _, name in ipairs(names) do
        print(greeter(name))
    end
end)
-- Execute all tasks in the scheduler
scheduler:runTasks()
```

In this example, the **TaskScheduler** object is defined using a table and metatable approach to simulate object-oriented behavior. The scheduler maintains a list of tasks, each added via **addTask** as a function. The tasks themselves can be closures that encapsulate their own state. One task counts from 1 to 3, and another uses a custom greeter function generated by **createGreeter**. By calling **runTasks**, the scheduler iterates through the task list and executes each task in sequence, demonstrating how closures and higher- order functions can be integrated into a modular and reusable code block.

This approach makes the code clearer and easier to maintain, and it's a great foundation for more complex programming tasks.

Debugging Advanced Lua Constructs

When working with such constructs, the control flow and variable states can become intricate, making it essential to have effective debugging strategies. We will learn to trace variable states and control flows, identify logical errors, and understand how different parts of our program interact. These techniques will help you quickly locate and fix issues, ensuring that our advanced Lua programs run as expected.

Tracing Variable States

A fundamental aspect of debugging is monitoring the values of variables during execution. When dealing with closures or functions that capture state, it can be challenging to know when and how these variables change. One common approach is to insert print statements strategically in our program code.

For example, if you have a closure that modifies its internal state, you might write:

```
function createAccumulator()
    local total = 0
    return function(amount)
        total = total + amount
        print("Accumulator state:", total)  -- Trace variable
state
        return total
    end
end
local accumulate = createAccumulator()
accumulate(5)     -- Output: Accumulator state: 5
accumulate(10)    -- Output: Accumulator state: 15
```

This prints the state of **total** each time the function is called, and you gain the insight into how the variable changes over time. This method is useful in complex loops or recursive functions, where a detailed trace of state changes is much needed for understanding the flow of execution.

Tracing Control Flow

When working with coroutines or nested functions, it's beneficial to trace control flow to see when certain functions are called or resumed. So in this, you can accomplish it by adding log messages at key points.

Let us say for example, we do debugging of a coroutine:

```
local function worker()
    print("Coroutine started.")
    for i = 1, 3 do
        print("Processing step", i)
        coroutine.yield()  -- Yield control back to the
scheduler
```

```
        print("Resuming at step", i)
    end
    print("Coroutine finished.")
end
local co = coroutine.create(worker)
print("Resuming coroutine first time:")
coroutine.resume(co)  -- Starts and yields
print("Resuming coroutine second time:")
coroutine.resume(co)  -- Resumes from first yield
print("Resuming coroutine third time:")
coroutine.resume(co)  -- Resumes again
print("Resuming coroutine final time:")
coroutine.resume(co)  -- Completes execution
```

In the above, the added print statements clarify the sequence of execution, revealing where the coroutine yields and resumes. This information is invaluable when tracking down issues in concurrent or iterative processes.

Utilizing Lua's Debug Library

Lua's built-in **debug** library offers additional tools for examining the internal state of our program. Functions like **debug.traceback** can help you obtain a stack trace when an error occurs, making it easier to pinpoint the source of the issue.

For example, you might catch errors in a higher- order function like this:

```
function safeCall(func, ...)
    local status, result = pcall(func, ...)
    if not status then
        print("Error encountered:")
        print(debug.traceback())
        return nil
    end
    return result
```

```
end
local function faultyFunction(x)
    return x + nil  -- Intentional error: cannot add number
and nil
end
safeCall(faultyFunction, 5)
```

When **faultyFunction** triggers an error, **debug.traceback** prints the call stack, giving you a clear picture of how the execution reached the problematic point. This level of detail is particularly useful for debugging deep call stacks and understanding the context in which errors occur.

Conditional Debug Logging

Sometimes, inserting print statements throughout our code can clutter our output, especially when debugging complex constructs. To manage this, you can implement a conditional debug logging function that only prints messages when debugging is enabled. For example:

```
local DEBUG = true
function debugLog(message)
    if DEBUG then
        print("[DEBUG]", message)
    end
end
function computeValue(a, b)
    debugLog("computeValue started with a = " .. tostring(a)
.. " and b = " .. tostring(b))
    local result = a * b + 10
    debugLog("computeValue result: " .. tostring(result))
    return result
end
computeValue(5, 3)
```

By controlling the **DEBUG** flag, you can easily turn debugging messages on or off, keeping our output clean during normal operation while providing detailed insights when troubleshooting.

Debugging Metatables and Overloaded Operators

When debugging constructs like metatables and operator overloading, issues can arise from incorrect metamethod definitions or improper attachment of metatables. To trace these issues, use **getmetatable** to verify that our objects have the expected metatable attached. For example:

```
local complex = { real = 2, imag = 3 }
local complexMeta = {
    __add = function(a, b)
        return { real = a.real + b.real, imag = a.imag +
b.imag }
    end
}
setmetatable(complex, complexMeta)
local mt = getmetatable(complex)
if mt and mt.__add then
    debugLog("Metatable attached correctly with __add
operator.")
else
    debugLog("Error: Metatable not set correctly.")
end
```

This bove program uses conditional logging to confirm that the metatable is present and contains the expected metamethods, helping you quickly identify integration issues in our custom data structures.

Through this topic, you learned various techniques for debugging advanced Lua constructs. By leveraging Lua's **debug** library, you acquired tools like **debug.traceback** to obtain detailed stack traces that are invaluable in identifying errors in deep call stacks. These debugging strategies provides a comprehensive framework for tackling complex Lua programs.

Summary

To sum up, you looked into advanced programming constructs that helped you learn more about what Lua can do. We learned how to use metatables and operator overloading, which let you change how tables behave and make objects that behaved in a way that you chose. We learned how to stop and change operations like addition and subtraction by doing them yourself. This gave you the freedom to model complex data interactions. We also learned more about coroutines and how to use them to do cooperative multitasking without using traditional threads.

You also looked into advanced function techniques and closures, which gave you the tools to build higher-order functions and encapsulate state. Lastly, you learned useful debugging skills for complex structures, with a focus on following variable states and control flow to quickly find and fix problems.

CHAPTER 5: PACKAGE MANAGEMENT AND MODULE CREATION

Overview

This chapter will teach you the basics of managing packages and making modules in Lua. First, you will learn about Luarocks, which is the official package manager for Lua modules and makes it easier to install and manage them. We are going to understand how Luarocks sets up and distributes modules, which will make adding libraries from other sources to our projects easier. To better manage dependencies and make our Lua apps more modular, you will find out why using a centralized system is an advantage.

Then you will see how to use Luarocks commands and configuration settings to install and manage modules. We will get better at looking for modules, installing them from repositories, and making sure they are up to date. We will learn how to fix installation problems and fix dependency conflicts by following along with examples. We will also learn how to make our own Lua modules, organize our code into parts that can be used again and again, and make our modules public so that other people can use them. This chapter teaches you how to keep the package ecosystem stable and safe, which will keep our Lua projects reliable and up to date.

Luarocks Overview

Luarocks Features

Luarocks offers a robust set of features to streamline module management for Lua programmers. With Luarocks, you can easily search for, install, update, and manage external libraries and modules, which can greatly simplify our development process. This tool helps you keep our projects organized and our dependencies under control, ensuring that our code remains modular, maintainable, and up to date.

Luarocks acts as a centralized repository and package management system for Lua modules. It allows you to access a vast collection of community-contributed modules that extend Lua's capabilities, from utility libraries and networking tools to complex frameworks and application-specific packages. Luarocks also supports version control, enabling you to specify and enforce version constraints for our modules. This means you can ensure compatibility between various parts of our project and avoid conflicts when updating dependencies. Moreover, Luarocks automates the process of module installation, updates, and dependency resolution, making it an essential tool for any serious Lua programmer.

Up and Running with Luarocks

To start using Luarocks, you first need to install it on our Linux system. Most distributions offer Luarocks in their package repositories, but you can also install it from source if you prefer the latest version or want to customize our installation.

For example, you can install Luarocks using following commands:

```
sudo apt update
sudo apt install luarocks
```

Once installed, you can verify that Luarocks is properly set up by checking its version:

```
luarocks --version
```

This command will display the version of Luarocks installed on our system, confirming that the installation process was successful. After installing Luarocks, you may need to update it from time to time. Keeping Luarocks current ensures that you benefit from the latest features and improvements, and it minimizes compatibility issues with newer modules.

Now, to update Luarocks, you can use our package manager if an update is available in the repository. Alternatively, if you installed Luarocks from source, you will need to download the latest version from the official website and follow the build instructions.

For example, if you installed from source, you can update Luarocks by running:

```
wget https://luarocks.org/releases/luarocks-<latest-version>.tar.gz
tar zxpf luarocks-<latest-version>.tar.gz
cd luarocks-<latest-version>
./configure; make; sudo make install
```

Here, replace **`<latest-version>`** with the current release number. This procedure downloads the latest tarball, extracts its contents, configures the build, and installs it. Through these commands, you will learn the process of compiling and installing software from source, which is a useful skill when packages are not available via our distribution's repositories.

Integrating Luarocks with Lua Projects

Once Luarocks is installed and updated, you will prepare it for use across our Lua projects. Luarocks integrates seamlessly with our Lua interpreter by installing modules into directories that Lua searches by default. This means you do not need to modify our code to require modules installed via Luarocks.

For example, if you want to install a popular module like **`lua-cjson`**, you simply execute:

```
luarocks install lua-cjson
```

The Luarocks will handle the download, compilation, and installation of the module. In our Lua script, you can then require the module as follows:

```
local cjson = require("cjson")
local data = { name = "Explorer", score = 95 }
local jsonString = cjson.encode(data)
print("JSON Output:", jsonString)
```

This above program demonstrates that you can use the installed module directly, without worrying about the underlying installation details.

In addition to installing and updating modules, you will also learn to manage dependencies effectively. Luarocks supports specifying version requirements for modules, for which you can define these dependencies in a configuration file or manage them through the command line. For example, if our project depends on a specific version of a module, you can enforce this by installing the required version:

```
luarocks install lua-cjson 2.1.0-1
```

This command installs version 2.1.0-1 of **lua-cjson**.

Through this topic, you gained comprehensive introduction to Luarocks and its vital role in Lua programming. This empowers you to manage dependencies effectively and build robust, modular applications with ease.

Installing and Managing Modules

Now that you've got the hang of Luarocks, it's time to put it into practice. You'll be installing modules, managing version dependencies, and configuring module settings using Luarocks commands. That way, you'll be able to integrate external libraries into our Lua projects seamlessly, making sure our code stays modular and easy to maintain.

Basic Module Installation

To get started, you just install a module using Luarocks. It's pretty simple: you run the install command followed by the module name.

For example, to install the popular JSON library **lua-cjson**, you type:

```
luarocks install lua-cjson
```

When you execute this command, Luarocks automatically downloads the module from its repository, compiles it if necessary, and installs it into the appropriate directory. After installation, you can verify its presence in our Lua environment by requiring it in our script:

```
local cjson = require("cjson")
local data = { name = "Explorer", score = 95 }
local jsonString = cjson.encode(data)
print("JSON Output:", jsonString)
```

This shows how installed modules become available to all Lua projects in order to extend functionality without reinventing the wheel.

Managing Version Dependencies

Sometimes, you need a specific version of a module to ensure compatibility with our project. Luarocks enables you to manage version dependencies by allowing you to specify the version when installing a module.

For example, if our project requires version 2.1.0-1 of **`lua-cjson`**, you can install it by running:

```
luarocks install lua-cjson 2.1.0-1
```

This command instructs Luarocks to fetch and install the specified version. If a newer version is available, our project will continue to use the version you explicitly installed, thus preventing unwanted changes that could break functionality.

You may also list installed modules and their versions using:

```
luarocks list
```

This command provides an overview of all modules managed by Luarocks, along with their installed versions to keep track of dependencies across the projects.

Configuring Module Settings

Some modules have configurable options that you can set through configuration files or environment variables. Although Luarocks mostly handles installation, you might need to adjust some module-specific settings to fit our project's needs. We can pass configuration parameters during initialization with some modules.

For example, if a module provides a settings table, you can configure it directly in our script:

```
local someModule = require("someModule")
-- Configure module settings by passing a configuration table
someModule.setup({
    option1 = true,
```

```
    option2 = "customValue",
    maxItems = 50
})
print("Module configured successfully.")
```

If the module documentation specifies configuration via environment variables, you can set these variables in our shell before running our Lua script:

```
export SOMEMODULE_OPTION1=true
export SOMEMODULE_MAXITEMS=50
lua your_script.lua
```

Using these methods, you ensure the module behaves as expected in our environment, and our configuration remains consistent across different systems.

Updating and Removing Modules

Over time, you may need to update modules to benefit from new features or security patches. Luarocks simplifies this by providing an update command. To update a module, you can run:

```
luarocks install lua-cjson --latest
```

This command checks for the latest version of the module and updates it if necessary. Similarly, if you want to remove a module that is no longer needed, you can use:

```
luarocks remove lua-cjson
```

These commands allow you to maintain a clean and current module ecosystem, which is crucial for long-term project stability.

Troubleshooting Module Installation

During installation or updates, you might encounter errors such as network issues, compilation failures, or conflicts with existing modules. In such cases, for example, if a dependency is missing, the error might indicate which library needs to be installed on our system. We may then install the required dependency using our package manager before retrying the Luarocks command.

If the error is related to version conflicts, consider specifying a compatible version or updating our project's dependency configuration. Additionally, Luarocks logs can provide insights into what went wrong during installation, so checking these logs may help you resolve the issue more efficiently.

Sample Program: Installing and Using a Module

To reinforce our learning, try installing another useful module, such as **luasocket**, which provides networking capabilities.

So first, install the module with:

```
luarocks install luasocket
```

Then, create a simple Lua script to test the module:

```
local socket = require("socket")
local host = "www.example.com"
local port = 80
-- Create a TCP connection to the host
local tcp = assert(socket.tcp())
tcp:connect(host, port)
tcp:send("GET / HTTP/1.1\r\nHost: " .. host .. "\r\n\r\n")
-- Receive the response and print it
local response, status = tcp:receive('*a')
print("Response from server:")
print(response)
tcp:close()
```

This teaches to use the **luasocket** module to establish a TCP connection, send a basic HTTP GET request, and print the server's response. Through this simple program, you practice both installing a module and incorporating it into our project.

Creating Custom Lua Modules

Designing Custom Module

SO far, we have very well understodd about the modules. Now to learn designing our own custom module, let us try to learn through one of our previous sample program, perhaps a simple calculator that performs basic arithmetic operations. In that, you can encapsulate these functions into a module.

Here, we begin with creating a new file named **calculator.lua**. In that file, you will define a table that will serve as our module and then add arithmetic functions to it.

```
-- calculator.lua
local calculator = {}
function calculator.add(a, b)
    return a + b
end
function calculator.subtract(a, b)
    return a - b
end
function calculator.multiply(a, b)
    return a * b
end
function calculator.divide(a, b)
    if b == 0 then
        return nil, "Division by zero error"
    end
    return a / b
end
return calculator
```

In the above module, you created a table called **calculator** and defined functions for addition, subtraction, multiplication, and division. Now here, you returned the **calculator** table at the end. This allowed other Lua files to load the module using the **require** function.

Integrating Custom Module

Once you have created our module, you can use it in our main application script by creating a new file, such as **main.lua**, and require the module to access its functions.

```
-- main.lua
-- Load the custom calculator module
local calc = require("calculator")
-- Use the module's functions
```

```
local sum = calc.add(10, 5)
local difference = calc.subtract(10, 5)
local product = calc.multiply(10, 5)
local quotient, errorMsg = calc.divide(10, 0)
print("Sum:", sum)
print("Difference:", difference)
print("Product:", product)
if quotient then
    print("Quotient:", quotient)
else
    print("Error:", errorMsg)
end
```

In this script, you load **`calculator.lua`** with **`require("calculator")`** and assign it to the variable **`calc`**. This makes all the functions defined in our module accessible through the **`calc`** table. We then perform arithmetic operations and print the results. Now here, if the error occurs in the division function, then you must print an appropriate message.

In summary, you learned to convert existing Lua scripts into custom modules and learned to define a module, load it using **`require`**, and integrate it into our project. This modular approach enhances the code organization, and also facilitates collaboration, testing, and future expansion of our ongoing Lua applications.

Summary

So, to sum up, you learned how to use Luarocks to manage packages and make modules. We studied how to use Luarocks as a powerful tool to find, install, and update Lua modules. This makes it easier to add libraries from outside our projects. We picked up how to install modules like lua-cjson and luasocket through hands-on activities and made sure they worked by adding them to sample programs. We saw how important version management was by giving exact module versions to keep things consistent and avoid problems with compatibility across different environments.

You also looked into ways to set module settings either directly through function calls or through environment variables, making sure that each module worked the way our project needed it to. We switched our attention from external modules to making our own custom modules, which turned Lua scripts that were once single-piece units into modular, self-contained parts. Overall, you improved our ability to handle dependencies well and encouraged the use of modules in software development.

Chapter 6: Popular Lua Modules and Extensions

Overview

This chapter will look at a number of well-known Lua modules and extensions that make the language more useful. We will look at modules that make HTTP communications easier, which lets you send and receive data quickly over the web. We will learn how to read and write JSON data, which is a very important skill for working with web APIs and other external data sources. We will get to know more about modules that let you connect to, query, and manage data in relational databases. These modules support database interactions. We will also look at file systems and utility modules, which are more powerful than the basic Lua I/O libraries and let you do more with files and the system.

Lastly, you will learn more about cryptography and security extensions. We will learn how to use encryption, decryption, and other safety measures to keep our apps safe. This chapter will teach you everything you need to know about how popular Lua modules can make our code much more useful, secure, and compatible with other programs.

HTTP Communications Modules

Overview of HTTP Modules

Several HTTP modules exist for Lua, each offering different features. LuaSocket's **`socket.http`** module is a popular choice due to its portability and ease of use. It provides basic functions for performing HTTP GET and POST requests, handling headers, and streaming responses. Other modules like lua-resty-http and lua-http provide additional features such as support for HTTP/2, asynchronous operations, or are optimized for specific environments like OpenResty. For this demonstration, you will work with LuaSocket because it is straightforward and widely supported.

In this section, you will learn about various HTTP modules available for Lua and then focus on practical integration using LuaSocket's HTTP module. This module allows you to send web requests, receive responses, and interact with remote APIs. We will explore how to set up requests, capture responses, and handle different HTTP methods, while gaining a solid understanding of how HTTP communication is achieved in Lua.

Basic HTTP GET Request

You start by setting up a simple HTTP GET request. In this example, you will request data from "http://httpbin.org/get", a service that returns request details in JSON format. LuaSocket's HTTP module works with the **`ltn12`** library to stream response data into a table.

The following program demonstrates this process in detail:

```
-- Require the necessary modules from LuaSocket
```

```
local http = require("socket.http")
local ltn12 = require("ltn12")
-- Create a table to store the response body
local response_body = {}
-- Build and send the HTTP GET request using a table as argument
local res, code, response_headers, status = http.request{
    url = "http://httpbin.org/get",
    sink = ltn12.sink.table(response_body),
    method = "GET"
}
-- Check if the request was successful
if code == 200 then
    print("HTTP GET request successful. Status code:", code)
    -- Combine the table elements to form the complete response string
    local full_response = table.concat(response_body)
    print("Response Body:")
    print(full_response)
else
    print("HTTP GET request failed. Status code:", code)
end
```

In the above program, you first require the **socket.http** and **ltn12** modules. We then create a table **response_body** that will hold the chunks of the response. The **http.request** function is used with a table of parameters including the URL, the sink function from **ltn12**, and the HTTP method. After the request, you check the returned status code and, if successful, concatenate the response chunks to display the full response.

Handling HTTP POST Requests

In addition to GET requests, you might need to perform POST requests to send data to a server. The process is similar but includes additional parameters like request body and headers.

Let us take a look at the below example where you perform an HTTP POST request:

```
local post_body = "name=LuaUser&age=30"
local response_body_post = {}
local res_post, code_post, headers_post, status_post =
http.request{
    url = "http://httpbin.org/post",
    method = "POST",
    headers = {
        ["Content-Type"] = "application/x-www-form-
urlencoded",
        ["Content-Length"] = tostring(#post_body)
    },
    source = ltn12.source.string(post_body),
    sink = ltn12.sink.table(response_body_post)
}
if code_post == 200 then
    print("HTTP POST request successful. Status code:",
code_post)
    local full_response_post =
table.concat(response_body_post)
    print("Response from POST request:")
    print(full_response_post)
else
    print("HTTP POST request failed. Status code:", code_post)
end
```

Here, you prepare a POST body with URL-encoded parameters. We specify HTTP headers such as **Content-Type** and **Content-Length** required by many servers. The request uses **ltn12.source.string** to stream the POST data and captures the response similarly to the GET request example.

Parsing and Processing API Responses

Often, web APIs return data in JSON format. Once you have captured the response, you may need to parse this JSON data into a Lua table for further processing. To achieve this, you can use the **lua-cjson** module.

The below program extends the previous GET request example to include JSON parsing:

```
local cjson = require("cjson")
local response_body = {}
local res, code, response_headers, status = http.request{
    url = "http://httpbin.org/get",
    sink = ltn12.sink.table(response_body)
}
if code == 200 then
    local full_response = table.concat(response_body)
    print("Raw JSON Response:")
    print(full_response)

    -- Parse JSON response into a Lua table
    local parsed_data = cjson.decode(full_response)
    -- Access a specific field, e.g., the URL from the JSON
response
    print("Extracted URL:", parsed_data.url)
else
    print("HTTP GET request failed. Status code:", code)
end
```

In this extended example, you require the **cjson** module and decode the JSON string obtained from the response into a Lua table. This enables you to easily access individual fields and integrate the API data into our application logic.

Advanced Request Customization

LuaSocket also allows for advanced customization of HTTP requests. We can set timeouts, add custom headers, and even handle redirects. For example, to set a timeout for our HTTP request, you can modify the request table:

```
local response_body = {}
local res, code, response_headers, status = http.request{
    url = "http://httpbin.org/get",
    sink = ltn12.sink.table(response_body),
    method = "GET",
    timeout = 10 -- timeout in seconds
}
if code == 200 then
    print("HTTP GET request successful with timeout. Status
code:", code)
    local full_response = table.concat(response_body)
    print("Response:")
    print(full_response)
else
    print("HTTP GET request failed or timed out. Status
code:", code)
end
```

Here, the **timeout** parameter ensures that if the server does not respond within 10 seconds, the request will fail, allowing our program to handle the timeout scenario gracefully.

Working with HTTPS

Although the examples above use HTTP, many APIs require HTTPS for secure communication. LuaSocket supports HTTPS if you have the appropriate LuaSec library installed. When using HTTPS, the process is similar, but you require the **ssl** module to secure the connection.

The following example on HTTPS might look like this:

```
-- Require LuaSocket's https and ltn12 modules (LuaSec
provides https)
local https = require("ssl.https")
local ltn12 = require("ltn12")
local response_body_https = {}
local res, code, response_headers, status = https.request{
```

```
    url = "https://httpbin.org/get",
    sink = ltn12.sink.table(response_body_https)
}
if code == 200 then
    local full_response = table.concat(response_body_https)
    print("HTTPS GET request successful. Status code:", code)
    print("Response:")
    print(full_response)
else
    print("HTTPS GET request failed. Status code:", code)
end
```

This example is nearly identical to the HTTP example, but it uses **`ssl.https`** to establish a secure connection. It ensures data transmitted between our application and the API endpoint remains encrypted.

Error Handling in HTTP Requests

When you're making HTTP requests, you might run into different issues like network timeouts, invalid URLs, or server errors. LuaSocket gives you an HTTP status code that you can check to see if the request was successful. We should also be able to handle nil responses gracefully.

For example, if the response is nil, you can print an error message:

```
local response_body = {}
local res, code, response_headers, status = http.request{
    url = "http://nonexistent.url/test",
    sink = ltn12.sink.table(response_body)
}
if not res then
    print("HTTP request error:", code)  -- code contains the
error message
else
    if code == 200 then
```

```lua
        print("Request succeeded.")
    else
        print("Request returned status code:", code)
    end
end
```

This error handling approach makes sure our application can react the right way when a request fails. All of this knowledge helps you build network-aware applications that can interact with remote APIs and handle various HTTP scenarios.

JSON Parsing and Serialization

JSON Parsing and Serialization is all about to convert Lua tables into JSON strings and back into Lua tables using JSON modules. This capability is essential when exchanging data between systems, particularly when interacting with web APIs or storing data in a platform-independent format. We will work with a popular JSON module, such as **lua-cjson**, to encode and decode JSON data. This makes possible to serialize Lua tables into a JSON format that can be transmitted over the network and then deserialize the JSON data back into Lua tables for further processing.

Converting Lua Tables to JSON Strings

So, to do this, you start by taking a Lua table, similar to one you may have used in previous examples. Suppose you have a table containing user information. Using the **lua-cjson** module, you can convert this table into a JSON string.

Following is a quick sample program:

```lua
-- Require the cjson module
local cjson = require("cjson")
-- Define a Lua table with user data
local user = {
    name = "Explorer",
    age = 30,
    interests = { "programming", "music", "travel" }
}
-- Convert the Lua table to a JSON string
```

```
local jsonString = cjson.encode(user)
print("JSON String:")
print(jsonString)
```

In this example, you load the **cjson** module and then encode the **user** table into a JSON string using **cjson.encode**. The printed JSON string represents the Lua table in a standard format that can be transmitted to other systems.

Reversing JSON Strings to Lua Tables

Once you have transmitted or stored JSON data, you may need to convert it back into a Lua table for further processing. This process is called deserialization. We will use the same **lua-cjson** module to decode a JSON string into a Lua table.

For this, let us consider the following example:

```
-- Assume jsonString contains a JSON string obtained from a remote system or file
local jsonString = '{"name":"Explorer","age":30,"interests":["programming","music","travel"]}'
-- Decode the JSON string back into a Lua table
local decodedUser = cjson.decode(jsonString)
-- Access fields from the decoded table
print("Decoded User Data:")
print("Name:", decodedUser.name)
print("Age:", decodedUser.age)
print("Interests:")
for index, interest in ipairs(decodedUser.interests) do
    print("  " .. index .. ":", interest)
end
```

Here, you decode the JSON string using **cjson.decode**, which converts the string back into a Lua table. We then access various fields, confirming that the data has been restored accurately. This deserialization process becomes very much essential when receiving data from web APIs, reading configuration files, or integrating with other systems that use JSON as their data format.

Integration for Data Exchange

If you combine serialization and deserialization, you can easily exchange data between systems. To give you an idea, let's say you need to send user data from our Lua application to a web service and then process the response. First, you'd convert our Lua table into JSON and send it via an HTTP POST request (like we talked about before), and then you'd get a JSON response. Lastly, you convert the response back into a Lua table for further analysis.

Given below is an integrated example that shows this data exchange in action:

```
local http = require("socket.http")
local ltn12 = require("ltn12")
local cjson = require("cjson")
-- Define a Lua table with user data to send to an API
local userData = {
    name = "Explorer",
    age = 30,
    interests = { "programming", "music", "travel" }
}
-- Serialize the Lua table to a JSON string
local jsonRequest = cjson.encode(userData)
print("Serialized JSON Request:")
print(jsonRequest)
-- Table to store the response body
local response_body = {}
-- Perform an HTTP POST request to a hypothetical API endpoint
local res, code, headers, status = http.request{
    url = "http://httpbin.org/post",
    method = "POST",
    headers = {
        ["Content-Type"] = "application/json",
        ["Content-Length"] = tostring(#jsonRequest)
```

```
    },
    source = ltn12.source.string(jsonRequest),
    sink = ltn12.sink.table(response_body)
}
if code == 200 then
    print("HTTP POST request successful. Status code:", code)
    local fullResponse = table.concat(response_body)
    print("Received JSON Response:")
    print(fullResponse)

    -- Deserialize the JSON response into a Lua table
    local decodedResponse = cjson.decode(fullResponse)


    -- Access specific parts of the response, for example, the
'json' field that httpbin.org returns
    if decodedResponse.json then
        print("Decoded Response Data:")
        print("Name:", decodedResponse.json.name)
        print("Age:", decodedResponse.json.age)
        print("Interests:")
        for i, interest in
ipairs(decodedResponse.json.interests) do
            print("  " .. i .. ":", interest)
        end
    else
        print("No JSON field found in the response.")
    end
else
    print("HTTP request failed with status code:", code)
```

```
end
```

In the above example, you combine the techniques of JSON parsing and serialization with HTTP communications. We encode a Lua table into a JSON string and send it via an HTTP POST request to a test API endpoint, http://httpbin.org/post. The API echoes back the JSON data, which you then decode back into a Lua table using **`cjson.decode`**.

Through these techniques, you can facilitate data exchange between different systems. Whether interacting with RESTful web services, storing configuration settings in a standard format, or exchanging information between Lua and other programming environments, JSON provides a versatile and widely supported format.

Database Interaction Modules

Sometimes, you've got to link a Lua application with a relational database, but that's not as easy as it sounds. You've got to use specialized modules to do it, and there's a module called LuaSQL that can connect to popular databases like MySQL, PostgreSQL, and SQLite.Now, we're going to look at how to set up a connection, run queries, handle transactions, and process results to manage dynamic data effectively. This'll show us how we can easily add database operations into our Lua programs, so we can build data-driven applications.

Connecting to Database

First, you'll need to set up a connection to a MySQL database using LuaSQL. To do that, you'll need to get the LuaSQL MySQL module and create an environment object in our Lua script. Then, you can use the environment to open a connection to our database by providing the necessary credentials, such as the database name, username, password, host, and port.

For example, the following code connects to a database named "testdb":

```
local luasql = require("luasql.mysql")
local env = luasql.mysql()
-- Connect to the database "testdb" with provided credentials
local con, err = env:connect("testdb", "user", "password",
"localhost", 3306)
if not con then
    print("Error connecting to database:", err)
    return
end
```

```
print("Connected to the database successfully.")
```

In this snippet, you create an environment and attempt to connect. Checking for errors immediately after connecting helps ensure that our application handles connection issues properly.

Executing Queries and Handling Transactions

After establishing the connection, you can execute SQL statements to manipulate and retrieve data. In this example, you create a table if it does not already exist, insert records into the table, and perform a query to retrieve data. LuaSQL's **execute** method is used to run SQL commands:

```
-- Create a table called 'users' if it doesn't exist
local res, err = con:execute([[
    CREATE TABLE IF NOT EXISTS users (
        id INT PRIMARY KEY AUTO_INCREMENT,
        name VARCHAR(100),
        age INT
    )
]])
if not res then
    print("Error creating table:", err)
end
-- Insert sample records into the 'users' table
con:execute("INSERT INTO users (name, age) VALUES ('Alice',
25)")
con:execute("INSERT INTO users (name, age) VALUES ('Bob',
30)")
-- Begin a transaction
con:execute("START TRANSACTION")
-- Update a record inside the transaction
con:execute("UPDATE users SET age = age + 1 WHERE name =
'Alice'")
-- Commit the transaction to save changes
```

```
con:execute("COMMIT")
```

This will help you create tables and insert data. You'll also learn how to manage transactions, like how to start a transaction, execute an update, and commit changes. All of these transactions make sure that multiple operations are done as one unit, which is important for keeping our data consistent.

Processing Query Results

Once you execute a SELECT query, you need to process the returned results. LuaSQL returns a cursor that you can iterate over to fetch each row as a Lua table. The following sample program shows how to fetch and print all records from the **users** table:

```
-- Execute a SELECT query to retrieve records from the 'users' table
local cur, err = con:execute("SELECT id, name, age FROM users")
if not cur then
    print("Error executing query:", err)
    return
end
print("Query Results:")
-- Fetch rows one by one using an associative array format
local row = cur:fetch({}, "a")
while row do
    print("ID: " .. row.id .. " | Name: " .. row.name .. " | Age: " .. row.age)
    row = cur:fetch(row, "a")
end
-- Close the cursor after processing the results
cur:close()
```

Here in the above, you iterate over the result set using a loop. Each row is printed, demonstrating how you can access fields by their column names. This allows you to dynamically process query results, integrate them into our application logic, or display them to users.

Once all database operations are complete, you should close both the connection and the environment:

```
-- Close the connection and environment
con:close()
env:close()
print("Database connection closed.")
```

When you close the connection and environment, you make sure our application doesn't have any open connections that could mess with database performance or lead to resource leaks.

File System and Utility Modules

In this topic, you will explore advanced file system and utility modules that enhance the basic file I/O operations you have learned earlier. While previous chapters introduced file reading and writing, here you will delve into modules that offer more robust file manipulation capabilities, detailed system monitoring, and resource management. One of the key modules for these purposes is LuaFileSystem (lfs), which provides functions to access file attributes, traverse directories, and interact with the file system in a more sophisticated manner.

LuaFileSystem for Advanced File Manipulation

LuaFileSystem (lfs) is a widely used module that gives you access to many files system-related operations. With lfs, you can retrieve file attributes (such as size, modification time, permissions, and file type), change the current working directory, and iterate over directory contents.

For instance, to get the attributes of a file, you can use:

```
local lfs = require("lfs")
-- Retrieve attributes of a specific file
local attr, err = lfs.attributes("example.txt")
if attr then
    print("File size:", attr.size)
    print("Modification time:", attr.modification)
    print("File mode:", attr.mode)
else
    print("Error getting attributes:", err)
end
```

In this example, lfs.attributes returns a table with various properties of the file "example.txt". We can use these properties to make decisions in our program, such as verifying file size or checking modification dates.

Directory Traversal and Listing Files

Another important aspect of file system manipulation is the ability to traverse directories and list their contents. Using the lfs.dir function, you can iterate over all items in a directory. This is useful for tasks such as searching for files that match a specific pattern or performing batch operations on a group of files.

```
local lfs = require("lfs")
local function listFiles(directory)
    print("Listing files in directory:", directory)
    for file in lfs.dir(directory) do
        if file ~= "." and file ~= ".." then
            local fullPath = directory .. "/" .. file
            local mode = lfs.attributes(fullPath, "mode")
            print("Found " .. mode .. ":", fullPath)
        end
    end
end
-- Call the function to list files in the current directory
listFiles(lfs.currentdir())
```

This code defines a function that lists each file and directory in the given path, excluding the current (`.`) and parent (`..`) directories. By combining lfs.dir with lfs.attributes, you can build complex file management utilities that process directories recursively or filter files based on type.

Advanced File Manipulation: Copying, Moving, and Deleting Files

While LuaFileSystem does not include built-in functions for copying or moving files, you can use Lua's os.execute function to call system commands or write our own file copy functions. For example, a simple approach to copy a file using Lua's I/O functions is as below:

```
local function copyFile(source, destination)
```

```
    local infile = io.open(source, "rb")
    if not infile then
        return nil, "Failed to open source file."
    end
    local outfile = io.open(destination, "wb")
    if not outfile then
        infile:close()
        return nil, "Failed to open destination file."
    end
    local content = infile:read("*all")
    outfile:write(content)
    infile:close()
    outfile:close()
    return true
end
local success, errMsg = copyFile("example.txt",
"example_copy.txt")
if success then
    print("File copied successfully.")
else
    print("Error copying file:", errMsg)
end
```

This function demonstrates a basic file copy operation by reading the entire contents of the source file and writing it to a destination file. For moving files, you could combine this copy function with a deletion step for the source file.

Similarly, deletion can be achieved with os.remove:

```
local removed, err = os.remove("example_copy.txt")
if removed then
    print("File deleted successfully.")
```

```
else
    print("Error deleting file:", err)
end
```

System Monitoring and Resource Management

Beyond file manipulation, utility modules also assist with system monitoring. LuaFileSystem provides the ability to check disk usage indirectly by reading file sizes and directory contents. We might also use Lua's os.execute to run shell commands for more comprehensive monitoring.

For example, to list disk usage, you could execute:

```
os.execute("df -h")
```

This command runs the system's disk free utility and displays disk usage statistics in a human-readable format. We can capture its output by redirecting it to a file or using io.popen to read the result:

```
local handle = io.popen("df -h")
local result = handle:read("*a")
handle:close()
print("Disk Usage Information:")
print(result)
```

Using io.popen, you can execute system commands and capture their output for processing within our Lua application. This method is useful for tasks like monitoring resource usage, generating reports, or triggering alerts based on system metrics.

Utility Functions for Enhanced File Management

In addition to LuaFileSystem, you may use utility functions to extend our file management capabilities. We can write functions to search for files matching specific patterns, recursively traverse directories, or even archive files.

For example, below is a simple function to search for files by extension:

```
local lfs = require("lfs")
local function searchFiles(directory, extension)
    local results = {}
```

```
    for file in lfs.dir(directory) do
        if file ~= "." and file ~= ".." then
            local fullPath = directory .. "/" .. file
            local mode = lfs.attributes(fullPath, "mode")
            if mode == "file" and file:match("%." .. extension
.. "$") then
                table.insert(results, fullPath)
            elseif mode == "directory" then
                local subResults = searchFiles(fullPath,
extension)
                for _, subFile in ipairs(subResults) do
                    table.insert(results, subFile)
                end
            end
        end
    end
    return results
end
local txtFiles = searchFiles(lfs.currentdir(), "txt")
print("Found text files:")
for _, filename in ipairs(txtFiles) do
    print(filename)
end
```

This function searches through a directory and its subdirectories for files with a specific extension. These utility functions are really helpful when managing large file systems or performing batch operations on a collection of files.

Sample Program: Directory Archiver

Below is a simplified example of a directory archiver. This script checks a specified directory for files not modified within the last day and moves them to an archive folder.

```
local lfs = require("lfs")
local os = require("os")
local function getModificationTime(filepath)
    local attr = lfs.attributes(filepath)
    return attr and attr.modification or nil
end
local function moveFile(source, destination)
    local infile = io.open(source, "rb")
    if not infile then return nil, "Unable to open source
file" end
    local outfile = io.open(destination, "wb")
    if not outfile then
        infile:close()
        return nil, "Unable to open destination file"
    end
    local content = infile:read("*all")
    outfile:write(content)
    infile:close()
    outfile:close()
    os.remove(source)
    return true
end
local function archiveOldFiles(directory, archiveDir, maxAge)
    local currentTime = os.time()
    for file in lfs.dir(directory) do
        if file ~= "." and file ~= ".." then
            local fullPath = directory .. "/" .. file
            local mode = lfs.attributes(fullPath, "mode")
            if mode == "file" then
```

```
                    local modTime = getModificationTime(fullPath)
                    if modTime and (currentTime - modTime >
maxAge) then
                        local destination = archiveDir .. "/" ..
file
                        local success, err = moveFile(fullPath,
destination)
                        if success then
                            print("Archived file:", fullPath,
"to", destination)
                        else
                            print("Failed to archive file:",
fullPath, "-", err)
                        end
                    end
                end
            end
        end
end
-- Define directories and maxAge (e.g., files older than 1
day)
local sourceDir = lfs.currentdir() .. "/data"
local archiveDir = lfs.currentdir() .. "/archive"
local oneDayInSeconds = 24 * 60 * 60
-- Create archive directory if it does not exist
if not lfs.attributes(archiveDir, "mode") then
    os.execute("mkdir " .. archiveDir)
end
-- Archive old files
archiveOldFiles(sourceDir, archiveDir, oneDayInSeconds)
```

In this example, the **archiveOldFiles** function checks each file in the specified directory. If the file's modification time is older than one day, it moves the file to an archive directory. The function **moveFile** performs a basic copy-and-delete operation. These techniques empower you to manage files and system resources in order to boost the functionality and robustness of our Lua applications.

Cryptography and Security Extensions

How Cryptography Secures Data?

Cryptography is essential for protecting sensitive data, ensuring that information remains confidential during storage and transmission. Cryptography modules secure data by transforming it from a readable format (plaintext) into an unreadable format (ciphertext) using a secret key and an IV. The encryption algorithm uses the key to scramble the data, and the IV ensures that identical plaintext blocks are encrypted into different ciphertext blocks, enhancing security. This process makes it nearly impossible for an attacker to derive the original data without access to the secret key.

Once the data is encrypted, even if it is intercepted during transmission or accessed without authorization, it remains protected because the decryption key is not known. Only someone with the correct key and IV can reverse the process and access the original information. This principle is critical for securing communications, such as when transmitting personal information over the internet or storing confidential data in a database.

Several cryptography modules are available for Lua, such as LuaCrypto, luaossl, and others. While LuaCrypto was popular in earlier versions, luaossl is a more modern library that leverages OpenSSL's extensive capabilities. Luaossl supports various cryptographic operations including hashing, encryption, and decryption. And for our practical learning and in this book, you will focus on luaossl as it provides a robust interface to OpenSSL.

In this section, we will use luaossl to demonstrate how symmetric encryption works, as the symmetric encryption uses the same key for both encrypting and decrypting data.

Luaossl for AES Encryption

To start, you need to have luaossl installed on our system. Once installed, you can require the module in our Lua script. In this demonstration, you will use the AES-256-CBC cipher, which is a widely recognized standard for secure encryption.

Below is a sample program that shows how to encrypt a plaintext message and then decrypt it back to its original form.

Setting up Cipher

At first, you begin with the luaossl module and retrieve the AES cipher. We must define a secret key and an initialization vector (IV). For AES-256, the key should be 32 bytes long, and for CBC mode, the IV should be 16 bytes long.

```
local openssl = require("openssl")
local cipher = openssl.cipher.get("aes-256-cbc")
-- Define a 32-byte key (ensure this is securely generated in real applications)
local key = "0123456789abcdef0123456789abcdef"
-- Define a 16-byte IV (also should be generated securely)
local iv = "abcdef9876543210"
-- The plaintext message that you want to secure
local plaintext = "Sensitive information: Do not share this data with unauthorized parties."
```

Encrypting Plaintext

Next, you encrypt the plaintext using the cipher's **encrypt** method. The method takes the plaintext, key, and IV as arguments and returns the ciphertext. In this sample, the encryption is performed in one step.

```
-- Encrypt the plaintext message
local encrypted = cipher:encrypt(plaintext, key, iv)
print("Encrypted Data:")
print(encrypted)
```

When this code is executed, the plaintext is transformed into a ciphertext, which appears as a garbled string. This encrypted output is what you would transmit over an insecure channel or store in a way that prevents unauthorized access.

Decrypting Ciphertext

To validate that the encryption was successful and reversible, you will decrypt the ciphertext using the same cipher, key, and IV. The decryption process should yield the original plaintext.

```
-- Decrypt the ciphertext back into plaintext
local decrypted = cipher:decrypt(encrypted, key, iv)
print("Decrypted Data:")
```

```
print(decrypted)
```

If the decryption is performed correctly, the output will match the original plaintext message. This confirms that the cryptographic process is working as intended.

Furthermore, always verify the integrity of the encrypted data. Techniques such as using cryptographic hash functions (e.g., SHA-256) can help ensure that the ciphertext has not been tampered with during transmission or storage.

Sample Program: Encrypting User Data for Transmission

Consider the following example that integrates JSON serialization with AES encryption, preparing data for secure transmission:

```
local openssl = require("openssl")
local cjson = require("cjson")
local cipher = openssl.cipher.get("aes-256-cbc")
-- Secure key and IV (in practice, generate these securely)
local key = "0123456789abcdef0123456789abcdef"
local iv = "abcdef9876543210"
-- Example Lua table with user data
local userData = {
    username = "SecureUser",
    email = "user@example.com",
    role = "admin"
}
-- Convert the Lua table to a JSON string
local jsonData = cjson.encode(userData)
print("JSON Data to Encrypt:")
print(jsonData)
-- Encrypt the JSON data
local encryptedData = cipher:encrypt(jsonData, key, iv)
print("Encrypted Data:")
print(encryptedData)
```

```
-- Simulate transmission here (e.g., send encryptedData over network)
-- Decrypt the received data
local decryptedJson = cipher:decrypt(encryptedData, key, iv)
print("Decrypted JSON Data:")
print(decryptedJson)
-- Convert JSON back to Lua table
local decodedData = cjson.decode(decryptedJson)
print("Decoded Lua Table:")
for k, v in pairs(decodedData) do
    print(k .. ":", v)
end
```

In this comprehensive example, you start with a Lua table containing user data. We then serialize the table into a JSON string using **`cjson.encode`**. The JSON string is encrypted using AES-256-CBC, resulting in ciphertext that can be safely transmitted. After simulating the transmission, the ciphertext is decrypted back to a JSON string and then deserialized into a Lua table using **`cjson.decode`**. The output shows each stage is secured during transmission and correctly restored on the receiving end.

By following these detailed examples, you learned how to integrate cryptography modules into our Lua applications to perform encryption and decryption. These techniques are fundamental for securing data transmissions and protecting sensitive information, ensuring that our applications remain resilient against unauthorized access.

Summary

By adding different Lua modules that made our application more useful, you broadened our programming skills. We learnt to make web requests, talk to remote APIs, and quickly process responses using HTTP modules. By using LuaSocket, you tried out the GET and POST operations, which are the building blocks of network communication. We also looked into JSON parsing and serialization, which let you change Lua tables into JSON strings and back again.

On top of that, you used special modules to connect our Lua programs to databases and run queries, handle transactions, and process results on the fly. We gained skills to work with relational databases and manage persistent data because of this experience. We also tried more advanced file system operations by using utility modules. Last but not least, you added security and cryptography features by including modules such as luaossl. We practiced using AES algorithms to encrypt and decrypt sensitive data, which kept the data safe while it was being sent. Overall, you came up with strong ways to handle errors and manage resources.

CHAPTER 7: WEB DEVELOPMENT WITH LAPIS

Overview

This chapter will teach you how to use the Lapis framework for web development. The Lapis framework is a powerful tool for making dynamic web apps that was built on Lua. It will teach you how to quickly set up Lapis in a Linux environment and give you a chance to use its powerful features. Next, you'll find out about some of the most important parts of Lapis development, such as routing, URL mapping, and how to render templates. We will see how to set up routes that connect certain URLs to Lua functions. This lets you respond to web requests in a dynamic way. We will also learn how to make and manage templates that separate presentation from business logic. This keeps the code clean and easy to maintain.

Lastly, you will look at managing sessions, integrating middleware, and putting Lapis apps into use. We will be taught to set up sessions for managing sessions and authenticating users. This will keep user data safe across multiple requests. Additional features, like logging and data validation, will be added by adding middleware components. We will find out about deployment strategies that will help you move our app from a development environment to production. We will learn how to build, secure, and deploy strong web apps using the Lapis framework by studying these topics.

Up and Running with Lapis Framework

Lapis Framework Overview

Lapis is an awesome web development framework built on Lua that makes it super easy to create dynamic, high-performance web applications. Lapis is all about making the most of Lua's simplicity and efficiency, giving you an organized structure and a syntax that's a breeze to use for building web applications.

Lapis is built to work seamlessly with Lua's lightweight nature. Its design focuses on modularity, allowing you to organize our code into logical sections such as controllers, models, and views. The framework provides a clear structure: the **`app`** directory houses our application logic (controllers and models), while the **`views`** directory contains our templates for rendering HTML responses. The configuration settings are defined in the **`config`** directory, which includes options for routing, database connections, and environment-specific settings. This clean separation of concerns enables you to build maintainable, scalable web applications and makes it easier to collaborate with other developers.

Lapis provides a range of built-in features that simplify common web development tasks. It offers an intuitive routing system that maps URLs to specific Lua functions, making it simple to handle different HTTP requests. Additionally, Lapis includes a robust template engine that allows you to generate dynamic HTML content by combining Lua logic with pre-designed templates. Its built-in support for session management and middleware integration means you can manage user sessions, authentication, and logging without relying on external libraries. These features come together to streamline the development process, letting you focus on writing our application's unique functionality rather than reinventing standard web components.

Initializing Lapis Project

Now that you understand what Lapis is and its key features, you will learn how to initialize a new project. With our current environment already equipped with Lua and LuaRocks, you can use Lapis's command-line tool to create a project scaffold.

You simply navigate to our desired workspace, then run:

```
lapis new my_project
cd my_project
```

This command creates a new directory called **my_project** that contains a pre-configured file structure. Inside this directory, you will find a **config.lua** file, an **app** folder for our controllers and models, and a **views** folder for our templates. By initializing a new project and examining the generated files, you set the stage for building dynamic web applications with Lua.

Routing and URL Mapping

In this topic, you will learn how to configure routing mechanisms in Lapis to handle web requests efficiently by mapping URLs to Lua functions. We will see how Lapis allows you to define clear pathways for incoming HTTP requests so that specific URLs trigger corresponding actions in our application. By working through practical examples, you will set up routes that link web addresses to Lua functions, which process the requests and generate appropriate responses.

Defining Routes

In Lapis, routes are typically defined in a central file, often within our **app** directory. We will create a Lua table where each key represents a URL pattern, and each value is a function that handles the request for that URL. For instance, you might define routes for the home page, a greeting page, and a dynamic user profile page.

Given below is an example that demonstrates the basic structure:

```
local lapis = require("lapis")
local app = lapis.Application()
-- Route for the home page
app:get("/", function(self)
```

```
  return { render = "index" }
end)
-- Route for a simple greeting page
app:get("/hello", function(self)
  return "Hello, welcome to our Lapis web app!"
end)
-- Route for a dynamic user profile using a URL parameter
app:get("/user/:id", function(self)
  local user_id = self.params.id
  return { render = "user", user = { id = user_id, name =
"User " .. user_id } }
end)
return app
```

In this code, you require the Lapis module and create an application instance. The **app:get** method defines a route for HTTP GET requests. For the home page ("/"), the route returns a render directive that tells Lapis to display the "index" template. For the **/hello** route, the function returns a simple text response. The dynamic route **/user/:id** demonstrates how to capture a parameter from the URL; here, **:id** is a placeholder that Lapis extracts and makes available through **self.params.id**. This implementation allows you to serve personalized content based on the URL.

Utilizing URL Parameters and Wildcards

Lapis supports the use of URL parameters and wildcards to handle a variety of routing scenarios. We learned that parameters, designated by a colon (**:**), allow you to extract specific parts of the URL. Wildcards can capture multiple segments.

For example, if you want to capture a nested path, you can use a wildcard parameter. See the example given below:

```
app:get("/files/*path", function(self)
  local file_path = self.params.path
  return "You requested the file at path: " .. file_path
end)
```

In this example, the ***path** wildcard captures all parts of the URL after **/files/**, storing the entire segment in **self.params.path**. This is particularly useful when you need to build file servers or create dynamic routes that can accept a variable number of subdirectories.

Mapping Routes to Template Rendering

In many web applications, you want to serve HTML pages by rendering templates with dynamic data. In Lapis, you can specify a render directive in our route's return value. For example, if you have a template named **index.lp**, you can instruct Lapis to render it by returning **{ render = "index" }**. Additionally, you can pass data to the template by including additional key-value pairs.

Following is a quick example around it:

```
app:get("/", function(self)
  local welcome_message = "Welcome to our Lapis application!"
  return { render = "index", message = welcome_message }
end)
```

When this route is called, Lapis will render the **index.lp** template and make the variable **message** available within the template. This allows you to separate the presentation logic from our routing logic and keep our code clean.

Configuring Routes for Multiple HTTP Methods

Lapis also lets you define routes for different HTTP methods (e.g., GET, POST, PUT, DELETE) so that the same URL can trigger different actions based on the type of request. For example, you might have one function that displays a form when a GET request is made, and another that processes the form data when a POST request is received:

```
-- Display the form using a GET request
app:get("/contact", function(self)
  return { render = "contact_form" }
end)
-- Process the form submission using a POST request
app:post("/contact", function(self)
  local name = self.params.name
  local email = self.params.email
```

```
    local message = self.params.message
    -- Process the submitted data, such as saving it to a
database
    return "Thank you, " .. name .. ", our message has been
received."
end)
```

Here, the **/contact** route handles two distinct actions based on the HTTP method. This approach allows you to build interactive applications where forms and other inputs are processed seamlessly.

Advanced Routing Patterns

As you build more complex web applications, you might need to define more advanced routing patterns. Lapis allows you to use regular expressions or multiple parameters in a single route to match complex URL structures.

For instance, if you want to capture both a category and an item identifier, you can define a route like this:

```
app:get("/shop/:category/:item_id", function(self)
    local category = self.params.category
    local item_id = self.params.item_id
    return { render = "item_detail", category = category,
item_id = item_id }
end)
```

In this scenario, the URL might look like **/shop/electronics/123**, and the route will extract the **category** as "electronics" and **item_id** as "123". This flexible routing mechanism allows you to structure our URLs logically and make our web application more intuitive to navigate.

Dynamic Routing and Middleware Integration

While defining routes, you can also integrate middleware functions to perform tasks such as authentication, logging, or data validation before the main route function executes. Middleware in Lapis can be added globally or to specific routes, ensuring that common tasks are handled uniformly across our application.

An example of integrating middleware might be:

```
local function require_authentication(self)
  if not self.session.user then
    return "Access denied", 403
  end
end
app:get("/dashboard", require_authentication, function(self)
  return { render = "dashboard" }
end)
```

In this code, the **require_authentication** function checks if a user session exists. If not, it returns an error message and a 403-status code. Otherwise, the dashboard route continues to render the appropriate template. This technique helps you manage security and other cross-cutting concerns without cluttering our route handlers.

Template Rendering Techniques

When building web applications, you often need to generate HTML that changes based on user input or data stored in our database. Instead of mixing Lua code directly with HTML strings, templates let you maintain a clear separation between the two. This separation ensures that our application logic remains independent from the design, which simplifies updates and allows designers and developers to work in parallel. With dynamic HTML content, you can render personalized pages, display lists of data, and adjust the presentation based on conditions in our application. The templating strategy you choose should make it easy to embed variables, control loops, and conditionals directly within the HTML code, thereby streamlining the generation of complex pages.

Templating in Lapis

Lapis provides a built-in templating engine that works with Lua, enabling you to write HTML templates that include Lua expressions. Templates are typically stored in the **views** directory of our project, and you can render them by returning a render directive from our route functions. Within these templates, you can insert dynamic values by using embedded Lua code. For instance, you can loop through a list of items, display conditional content, or include partial templates to reuse common components. This keeps our routing and business logic separate from our presentation layer to improve the overall structure and maintainability of our web application.

Sample Program: Template Rendering

Suppose you have a simple web application that displays a list of products. We can create a template named **`products.lp`** in the **`views`** directory. The template might look like this:

```
<!DOCTYPE html>
<html>
<head>
  <meta charset="UTF-8">
  <title>Product List</title>
</head>
<body>
  <h1>Available Products</h1>
  <ul>
    <% for i, product in ipairs(products) do %>
      <li>
        <strong><%= product.name %></strong> - $<%=
product.price %>
      </li>
    <% end %>
  </ul>
</body>
</html>
```

In this template, **`<% ... %>`** is used for Lua control structures, and **`<%= ... %>`** is used to output variables. When this template is rendered, the Lua code within the tags is executed, and the resulting HTML is sent to the client.

Next, in our route file, you can set up a route that prepares the data and instructs Lapis to render the template as shown below:

```
local lapis = require("lapis")
local app = lapis.Application()
app:get("/products", function(self)
  local products = {
    { name = "Laptop", price = 999.99 },
```

```
    { name = "Smartphone", price = 499.99 },
    { name = "Tablet", price = 299.99 }
  }
  -- Render the 'products' template, passing the products
table
  return { render = "products", products = products }
end)
return app
```

Here, you create an array of product tables and pass it to the template via the return value. When the route is accessed, Lapis renders the **products.lp** template. The template iterates over the products table and dynamically generates an HTML list, where each product's name and price are displayed.

Separating Business Logic from Presentation

With templates in our Lapis application, you can make sure that our business logic—like data fetching and processing—stays in the Lua route functions, and the presentation details are limited to the template files. This design keeps our code clean and easier to maintain. For example, if you decide to change the layout of the product list later, you only need to modify the template file without changing the underlying logic that prepares the product data. And if you want to enhance the application's functionality by fetching products from a database, you can update the route handler while leaving the template intact. This modular approach makes it simpler to test, update, and scale our web application over time. During this topic, you practiced generating dynamic HTML content using Lapis's templating engine. We learned how to embed Lua code within HTML to create loops and insert variables, which allows you to produce personalized and data-driven pages. We also saw how keeping the business logic separate from the presentation clarifies the code structure and enhances collaboration and future maintenance.

Session Management and Middleware

We'll go over how to set up session tracking and integrate middleware in our Lapis application.When you add session management, you can keep track of user information like their authentication status across multiple requests.On the other hand, middleware lets you inject custom logic—like logging or authentication checks—into the requests.These features help you build secure and reliable web applications that respond correctly to user actions.

Implementing Session Tracking

Lapis provides built-in session management that is easy to set up and use. Once configured in our **config.lua** file, sessions allow you to store user-specific data. For instance, you might store authentication tokens or user preferences. In our route functions, you can access the session using **self.session** to set or retrieve values.

Below is an example route that demonstrates session usage in a simple login scenario:

```
local lapis = require("lapis")
local app = lapis.Application()
-- Route to display the login form
app:get("/login", function(self)
  return { render = "login" }
end)
-- Route to process the login form
app:post("/login", function(self)
  local username = self.params.username
  local password = self.params.password

  -- In a real scenario, verify credentials against a database
  if username == "user" and password == "secret" then
    -- Store user information in session
    self.session.user = { username = username }
    return "Login successful. Welcome, " .. username .. "!"
  else
    return "Invalid credentials. Please try again."
  end
end)
-- Route to display a protected page that requires
authentication
app:get("/dashboard", function(self)
  if not self.session.user then
    return "Access denied. Please log in."
```

```
  end
  return "Welcome to our dashboard, " ..
self.session.user.username .. "!"
end)
return app
```

In the above program, the GET **/login** route renders a login form (template not shown here). The POST **/login** route processes form submissions and, upon successful authentication, stores a user object in the session. The **/dashboard** route checks the session for a user; if not found, it denies access. By using sessions, you ensure that a user's authentication state persists across requests.

Integrating Middleware for Authentication and Logging

You can use middleware in Lapis to run code before or after our route handlers. That way, you can combine common tasks, like authentication checks and logging. We can add middleware in Lapis to our whole application or just to certain routes.

For example, to make sure the user is logged in on certain routes, you can write a middleware function that checks if the user is logged in:

```
local function require_authentication(self)
  if not self.session.user then
    return { status = 403, "Access denied. Please log in." }
  end
end
-- Apply the middleware to a route
app:get("/profile", require_authentication, function(self)
  return "User Profile for " .. self.session.user.username
end)
```

Here, the **require_authentication** middleware is executed before the **/profile** route. If the session does not contain a user, the middleware returns an error message with a 403 status code, preventing the route handler from executing. This pattern allows you to secure multiple routes by applying the same middleware function.

Similarly, for logging purposes, you can create a middleware that logs details about each request, such as the URL accessed and the timestamp. Following is the best example to understand it better:

```
local function request_logger(self)
  local timestamp = os.date("%Y-%m-%d %H:%M:%S")
  print("[" .. timestamp .. "] " .. self.req.method .. " " ..
self.req.path)
end
-- Global middleware to log every request
app:before_filter(request_logger)
```

The **before_filter** function in Lapis allows you to register a middleware that executes before every request is processed. In the **request_logger** middleware, you print the current timestamp along with the HTTP method and path of the request.

Combining Session Management and Middleware

The integration of session management with middleware creates a robust foundation for secure and maintainable web applications. Consider a scenario where you need to both authenticate users and log every request wherein you can combine the previously defined middleware functions to achieve this:

```
-- Global logging middleware
app:before_filter(function(self)
  local timestamp = os.date("%Y-%m-%d %H:%M:%S")
  print("[" .. timestamp .. "] " .. self.req.method .. " " ..
self.req.path)
end)
-- Middleware for routes that require authentication
local function require_authentication(self)
  if not self.session.user then
    return { status = 403, "Access denied. Please log in." }
  end
end
-- Protected route with both session check and logging
app:get("/settings", require_authentication, function(self)
```

```
  return "User Settings for " .. self.session.user.username
end)
```

As shown above, the global logging middleware logs every request. The **/settings** route uses the **require_authentication** middleware to ensure that only logged-in users can access the settings page. If the user is authenticated, the route handler executes and returns a personalized response.

When working with sessions and middleware in Lapis, you will typically configure session management in our configuration file. This configuration determines how sessions are stored (e.g., in cookies, on the server side, etc.) and any related parameters such as session expiration. Although you do not need to delve into those details here, it is important to understand that session handling can be customized according to our application's needs. Similarly, middleware functions should be designed to be lightweight and efficient, as they run on every request (in the case of global middleware) or on a set of routes.

Deploying Lapis Applications

To prepare and deploy our Lapis-based web applications into production environments, you need to transition from a development environment to a live server setup. For doing this, tasks like making configuration adjustments, selecting a suitable production server, and employing deployment tools are needed to perform in order to ensure our application runs smoothly and securely.

Preparing Application for Production

Before deploying our application, you need to ensure that our code is production-ready. We will start by verifying that all features are functioning as expected in our local environment. Next, review our project's configuration, particularly the settings in our **config.lua** file. When you're in production, you might need to tweak some settings like the server port, database connections, and session handling to make sure everything works right in the target environment. It's super important to get rid of any development-specific code or debugging statements to keep our application clean and organized. And don't forget to make sure any sensitive info, like API keys or database credentials, is stored safely. We can do this by using environment variables or configuration files that aren't included in version control.

Adjusting Configuration for Production

After this, we may need to change several configuration settings. For example, you might switch from a development environment to a production environment by modifying the environment variable in our configuration. Lapis allows you to specify different settings based on the environment. Ensure that logging is set appropriately, and consider enabling features that enhance security, such as session encryption and stricter error reporting. In our configuration file, you can define parameters such as:

```
return {
  port = 8080,
  environment = "production",
  database = {
    host = "prod.db.server",
    name = "prod_db",
    user = "prod_user",
    password = "secure_password"
  }
}
```

These settings ensure that our application connects to the correct database and listens on the appropriate port in production. But remember, that we need to update these configurations based on our hosting environment.

Choosing a Production Server

Choosing the right production server is super important for a successful deployment, and we're here to help you make the best choice! You might choose a dedicated server, a virtual private server (VPS), or a cloud-based platform such as AWS, DigitalOcean, or Linode. The great news is that Lapis applications can run on any server that supports Lua and OpenResty. Often, production deployments use Nginx in conjunction with OpenResty to serve the application. If you go with OpenResty, you'll get awesome features like Lua code caching and enhanced security controls. To get our server ready, all you'll need to do is install the necessary dependencies.

Deployment Workflow and Tools

To deploy our Lapis application, you may use a version control system, such as Git, to manage our codebase. Once our application is pushed to a repository, you can pull the latest changes on our production server. There are tools like Docker which can help containerize our application to build consistency between development and production environments.

Now here, a typical workflow might involve:

1. **Push Code to Repository**
2. **Pull Code on Production Server**

3. **Install Dependencies**
4. **Adjust Configuration**

After this, just launch our Lapis server, either directly or using a process manager such as Supervisor or systemd to keep our application running continuously. For example, on our production server, you might run:

```
git pull origin main
luarocks install --only-deps .
lapis server production
```

This set of commands pulls the latest code, installs necessary dependencies, and starts the Lapis server in production mode. Once our application is deployed, you need to monitor its performance and ensure that it remains secure. This process gets you skilled to manage real-world deployments to let application runs securely and efficiently.

Summary

To sum up what we learned in this chapter, you now have a solid understanding of how to use the Lapis framework to build web applications. First, you looked at Lapis's structure and picked up how to divide our project into controllers, views, and configuration files. Next, you started a new project with a scaffold that was ready to use. We set up a development server locally and made sure our app was running correctly. After that, you made more complex routing systems that connected URLs to specific Lua functions. We discovered how to use URL parameters and wildcards to get data from the client side and process it.

You understood to make dynamic HTML content by using Lapis's built-in templating engine to separate our business logic from the presentation. We made templates with Lua expressions that let content be rendered dynamically. We also added middleware and session management to our app, which let you keep track of user sessions and make sure they were safe by authenticating them and logging their activities. Lastly, you got our app ready for production by making changes to the settings and deploying it using modern workflows for deployment. Overall, you learned how to use Lapis to build, secure, and deploy scalable web applications, which gave you the skills to make interactive and reliable web solutions.

Chapter 8: Embedding Lua in JavaScript Apps

Overview

This chapter will teach you how to connect Lua and JavaScript so that you can use Lua in JavaScript environments to make web apps better. We will find out about ways to connect Lua and JavaScript and how to call Lua functions from JavaScript and JavaScript functions from Lua. This chapter also talks about ways to embed Lua directly in web pages so that you can run Lua scripts in the browser.

Then you can discover how to exchange and change data between Lua and JavaScript. We will explore how to convert data structures smoothly so that data can flow between the two languages without any problems. We will be discovering how to improve performance with Lua by doing things like giving computational tasks to Lua to make JavaScript apps more responsive. This integration not only improves performance, but it also gives you a flexible way to handle complex tasks and data processing in our web projects.

Additionally, you will use these methods to create hybrid apps that use both Lua's speed and JavaScript's flexibility. This chapter gives you useful tips on how to handle changing data, improve performance, and make it easier for Lua and JavaScript to talk to each other.

Interfacing Lua and JavaScript

First, let's appreciate that Lua isn't confined to just standalone scripts or embedded systems—it can also run in the browser alongside JavaScript. Fengari, a Lua VM written in JavaScript, lets you execute Lua code directly on a webpage. Picture our web page as a canvas where both Lua and JavaScript can work in harmony.

To understand better, let us think as if you're working on a modern web application where JavaScript drives the front end, and you want to harness Lua's computational power right within our browser. We will see how you can bridge these two worlds using a binding library called Fengari. In the below, we will build a live demonstration to interface Lua with JavaScript.

Setting up Environment Live

You go onto the HTML file and add this script tag to load Fengari:

```
<script src="https://unpkg.com/fengari-web/dist/fengari-
web.js"></script>
```

This step brings Lua right into our browser. With Fengari loaded, you're now ready to mix Lua into our JavaScript code.

Running Lua Code

Let's write a simple Lua function that greets a user. Create a Lua script as a string:

```
-- Lua code as a string
function greet(name)
  return "Hello, " .. name .. " from Lua!"
end
```

Now, switch over to our JavaScript console and run the following:

```
// Initialize the Lua state using Fengari
const { lua, lauxlib, lualib } = fengari;
const L = lauxlib.luaL_newstate();
lualib.luaL_openlibs(L);
// Define the Lua script as a string
const luaScript = `
  function greet(name)
    return "Hello, " .. name .. " from Lua!"
  end
`;
// Load and run the Lua script
if (lauxlib.luaL_loadstring(L, luaScript) === lua.LUA_OK) {
  if (lua.lua_pcall(L, 0, 0, 0) !== lua.LUA_OK) {
    console.error("Lua error:", lua.lua_tojsstring(L, -1));
  }
}
```

Watch the console: nothing unexpected appears yet—that's because we've just loaded the Lua function.

Calling Lua from JavaScript

Next, let's call the Lua function directly from JavaScript. We push the function onto the Lua stack, pass a parameter, and capture the result:

```
// Push the Lua function 'greet' onto the stack
lua.lua_getglobal(L, "greet");
```

```
// Pass an argument to the Lua function
lua.lua_pushstring(L, "JavaScript User");
// Call the Lua function (1 argument, 1 return value)
if (lua.lua_pcall(L, 1, 1, 0) !== lua.LUA_OK) {
  console.error("Error calling greet:", lua.lua_tojsstring(L,
-1));
} else {
  // Retrieve and print the result
  const result = lua.lua_tojsstring(L, -1);
  console.log("Greeting from Lua:", result);
  lua.lua_pop(L, 1); // Clean up the stack
}
```

As you run this, notice the greeting appears in our JavaScript console. This live interaction shows how seamlessly Lua functions can be invoked from JavaScript.

Managing Data Exchange

To further demonstrate data exchange, imagine you have a Lua function that sums an array of numbers. Write this Lua code:

```
function sumNumbers(numbers)
  local sum = 0
  for i = 1, #numbers do
    sum = sum + numbers[i]
  end
  return sum
end
```

Then, in JavaScript, pass an array to Lua by constructing a Lua table:

```
// Define a JavaScript array
const numbers = [10, 20, 30, 40];
// Create a new Lua table and populate it with numbers
```

```
lua.lua_newtable(L);
numbers.forEach((num, index) => {
  lua.lua_pushnumber(L, num);
  lua.lua_rawseti(L, -2, index + 1);
});
// Set the table as a global variable 'numList'
lua.lua_setglobal(L, "numList");
// Load and execute Lua code to call sumNumbers on 'numList'
const luaSumScript = `
  local result = sumNumbers(numList)
  return result
`;
if (lauxlib.luaL_loadstring(L, luaSumScript) === lua.LUA_OK) {
  if (lua.lua_pcall(L, 0, 1, 0) !== lua.LUA_OK) {
    console.error("Error computing sum:",
lua.lua_tojsstring(L, -1));
  } else {
    const totalSum = lua.lua_tonumber(L, -1);
    console.log("Sum computed by Lua:", totalSum);
    lua.lua_pop(L, 1);
  }
}
```

This creates a Lua table from our JavaScript array, calls the Lua **sumNumbers** function, and retrieves the computed sum. With this, you witnessed a live integration of Lua within a JavaScript environment using Fengari. This highlights how you can leverage Lua's simplicity and power directly in our JavaScript applications for performance optimization and advanced computational tasks.

Embedding Lua in Web Pages

We now extend the integration of Lua and JavaScript by embedding Lua scripts directly into our web pages. This method allows you to execute Lua code within the browser context, enhancing client-side interactivity and performance.

Let's start by creating a simple HTML page that loads Fengari, the Lua virtual machine implemented in JavaScript. This will allow you to run Lua code right in our browser. Then, go to our favorite text editor and create an HTML file with the following content:

```
<!DOCTYPE html>
<html>
<head>
  <meta charset="UTF-8">
  <title>Lua Embedded in Web Page</title>
  <!-- Load Fengari library -->
  <script src="https://unpkg.com/fengari-web/dist/fengari-
web.js"></script>
</head>
<body>
  <h1>Dynamic Content with Lua</h1>
  <div id="output">Loading...</div>
  <script>
    // Initialize Fengari and create a new Lua state
    const { lua, lauxlib, lualib } = fengari;
    const L = lauxlib.luaL_newstate();
    lualib.luaL_openlibs(L);
    // Define a Lua script as a string. This script generates
dynamic content.
    const luaScript = `
      function generateContent()
        local message = "Hello from Lua embedded in a web
page!"
        local items = { "Item 1", "Item 2", "Item 3", "Item 4"
}
        local content = "<p>" .. message .. "</p><ul>"
```

```
      for i = 1, #items do
        content = content .. "<li>" .. items[i] .. "</li>"
      end
      content = content .. "</ul>"
      return content
    end
  `;
  // Load and execute the Lua script
  if (lauxlib.luaL_loadstring(L, luaScript) === lua.LUA_OK)
{
    if (lua.lua_pcall(L, 0, 0, 0) !== lua.LUA_OK) {
      console.error("Error executing Lua script:",
lua.lua_tojsstring(L, -1));
    }
  } else {
    console.error("Error loading Lua script:",
lua.lua_tojsstring(L, -1));
  }
  // Call the Lua function 'generateContent' to produce
dynamic HTML
  lua.lua_getglobal(L, "generateContent");
  if (lua.lua_pcall(L, 0, 1, 0) !== lua.LUA_OK) {
    console.error("Error calling generateContent:",
lua.lua_tojsstring(L, -1));
  } else {
    // Retrieve the returned HTML string from Lua
    const dynamicContent = lua.lua_tojsstring(L, -1);
    // Insert the dynamic content into the page
    document.getElementById("output").innerHTML =
dynamicContent;
    lua.lua_pop(L, 1);
```

```
    }
  </script>
</body>
</html>
```

In this demonstration, you first load Fengari from a CDN. Within the **<script>** tag, you initialize a Lua state and open the standard libraries. We then define a Lua function named **generateContent** that builds an HTML string with a message and a list of items. This function uses a loop to iterate over a table and constructs a dynamic HTML structure.

After defining the Lua script as a string, you load and execute it within the Lua state. If the script loads successfully, you call the **generateContent** function. The Lua function returns a complete HTML string which is then extracted from the Lua state using Fengari's API. Finally, you update a **<div>** element with the ID **output** in our HTML, replacing its content with the generated HTML.

This integration supports advanced dynamic functionalities, such as generating personalized content or processing data on the fly, all within the client-side environment. The result is a more interactive and responsive web application.

Data Exchange and Transformation

Building on the previous example where Lua was embedded in our web page, you will now focus on converting data structures between the two languages. This allows you to validate, manipulate, and ultimately render dynamic content based on the exchanged data.

Preparing Data in Lua

Imagine you have a Lua function that prepares data to be sent to JavaScript. In this demonstration, you will create a Lua table containing user details and then convert it into a JSON string so that JavaScript can easily consume it. The Lua code snippet below defines a function that creates a user data table and serializes it to JSON using a Lua JSON module such as lua-cjson.

```
-- Lua code to create and serialize user data
local cjson = require("cjson")
function getUserData()
  local user = {
    username = "LuaLover",
    age = 28,
```

```
    interests = { "coding", "reading", "gaming" }
  }
  -- Serialize the table to a JSON string
  local jsonData = cjson.encode(user)
  return jsonData
end
```

Here, you create a user table and use **cjson.encode** to convert it into a JSON formatted string. This JSON string can then be passed back to JavaScript, where it can be parsed and used to update the user interface.

Passing Data from Lua to JavaScript

Now we will use Fengari, and with it, we can call the Lua function from JavaScript and retrieve the JSON string. In the previous section, you saw how to execute Lua code in the browser. Now, let's extend that to exchange data.

In our JavaScript code, after setting up the Lua state, call the **getUserData** function and capture its output.

```
// JavaScript code snippet using Fengari to call getUserData
// Push the Lua function 'getUserData' onto the Lua stack
lua.lua_getglobal(L, "getUserData");
// Call the function with 0 arguments expecting 1 result
if (lua.lua_pcall(L, 0, 1, 0) !== lua.LUA_OK) {
  console.error("Error calling getUserData:",
lua.lua_tojsstring(L, -1));
} else {
  // Retrieve the JSON string from the Lua stack
  const userJson = lua.lua_tojsstring(L, -1);
  console.log("Received JSON from Lua:", userJson);
  lua.lua_pop(L, 1);

  // Parse the JSON string into a JavaScript object
```

```
  const userData = JSON.parse(userJson);
  console.log("Parsed User Data:", userData);
}
```

Here, you call the Lua function **getUserData** and obtain a JSON string. The JSON string is then parsed into a JavaScript object using **JSON.parse()**, making it easy to access individual properties such as **username**, **age**, and **interests**.

Validating and Transforming Data

Once the data is in JavaScript, you may need to validate and transform it before using it in our application. For instance, you might check if the age is within a certain range or format the list of interests for display.

Given below is an example of data validation and transformation in JavaScript:

```
// Validate the received user data
if (userData.age < 18) {
  console.warn("User is underage!");
} else {
  console.log("User age is valid.");
}
// Transform interests into an HTML list
let interestsHtml = "<ul>";
userData.interests.forEach(function(interest) {
  interestsHtml += "<li>" + interest.charAt(0).toUpperCase() +
interest.slice(1) + "</li>";
});
interestsHtml += "</ul>";
// Inject the transformed data into the web page
document.getElementById("user-interests").innerHTML =
interestsHtml;
```

Here, you first check the user's age and output a warning if they are underage. Then, you iterate over the interest array, transforming each interest by capitalizing the first letter and wrapping it in an HTML list item. Finally, you combine the list items into a single HTML unordered list and insert it into the page. This live transformation ensures that raw data from Lua is converted into a user-friendly format for display.

Data Exchange from JavaScript to Lua

The great thing about this exchange is that it's a two-way street! You've got the power to send data from JavaScript to Lua for processing, and it's just as easy to send data from Lua to JavaScript. Now, if you want to send JavaScript object to Lua, then you'll convert the object into a JSON string. Then, you'll push that string into the Lua state, where Lua can decode it back into a table.

```
// JavaScript object to send to Lua
const newUser = {
  username: "JSWarrior",
  age: 35,
  interests: ["hiking", "coding", "photography"]
};
// Convert JavaScript object to JSON string
const newUserJson = JSON.stringify(newUser);
// Push the JSON string into Lua
lua.lua_pushstring(L, newUserJson);
lua.lua_setglobal(L, "newUserJson");
```

In Lua, you can then decode this JSON string back into a table using the **cjson** module:

```
-- In Lua, decode the JSON string passed from JavaScript
local newUserData = cjson.decode(newUserJson)
print("New user data received from JavaScript:")
print("Username: " .. newUserData.username)
print("Age: " .. newUserData.age)
for i, interest in ipairs(newUserData.interests) do
  print("Interest " .. i .. ": " .. interest)
end
```

This round-trip data exchange enables you to harness the strengths of both Lua and JavaScript. We can perform heavy computations or data processing in Lua, then pass the results to JavaScript for updating the UI, or vice versa.

During our development process, it's so important to see real-time feedback when the data is exchanged and transformed. We can use browser consoles and Lua print statements to log data at each step. This live debugging helps make sure that the data is correctly formatted and that any transformation logic is working as expected. For example, if the JSON parsing fails or data values are unexpected, you can log error messages and adjust our transformation logic.

Performance Enhancements

We all know that Lua is awesome because it's so lightweight and fast. That makes it perfect for those really demanding tasks that need top-notch performance. When you bring Lua into our JavaScript environment with Fengari, you can set up a special Lua state to do those tricky calculations without holding up the main JavaScript thread.This way, Lua can do its thing in the background, crunching numbers, while our JavaScript code stays nice and responsive to whatever the user is doing. For example, imagine you need to calculate the sum of a large array of numbers or run a simulation with lots of iterative computations.

Performing Heavy Computation

Suppose you need to compute the sum of the squares of the first N numbers, where N is large. Instead of running this loop in JavaScript, you write a Lua function to handle the computation.

Given below is the Lua code as a string:

```
-- Lua code for heavy computation: sum of squares
function computeSumOfSquares(n)
  local sum = 0
  for i = 1, n do
    sum = sum + i * i
  end
  return sum
end
```

This function iterates from 1 to N, squaring each number and accumulating the result. In a computationally intensive scenario, such a loop could be performance-critical if executed frequently.

Integrating Lua into JavaScript for Computation

Next, you embed this Lua function into our JavaScript application using Fengari. In our HTML file, ensure Fengari is loaded as shown previously:

```
<script src="https://unpkg.com/fengari-web/dist/fengari-
web.js"></script>
```

Then, in our JavaScript code, set up the Lua state, load the Lua script, and call the function with a large value for N:

```
// Initialize Fengari components
const { lua, lauxlib, lualib } = fengari;
const L = lauxlib.luaL_newstate();
lualib.luaL_openlibs(L);
// Define the Lua script as a string for heavy computation
const luaScript = `
  function computeSumOfSquares(n)
    local sum = 0
    for i = 1, n do
      sum = sum + i * i
    end
    return sum
  end
`;
// Load and execute the Lua script
if (lauxlib.luaL_loadstring(L, luaScript) === lua.LUA_OK) {
  if (lua.lua_pcall(L, 0, 0, 0) !== lua.LUA_OK) {
    console.error("Error executing Lua script:",
lua.lua_tojsstring(L, -1));
  }
} else {
  console.error("Error loading Lua script:",
lua.lua_tojsstring(L, -1));
}
```

```
// Function to call Lua's computeSumOfSquares from JavaScript
function calculateSumOfSquares(n) {
  // Push the function onto the Lua stack
  lua.lua_getglobal(L, "computeSumOfSquares");
  // Push the argument n onto the Lua stack
  lua.lua_pushnumber(L, n);
  // Call the function (1 argument, 1 result)
  if (lua.lua_pcall(L, 1, 1, 0) !== lua.LUA_OK) {
    console.error("Error calling computeSumOfSquares:",
lua.lua_tojsstring(L, -1));
    return null;
  }
  // Retrieve the result from Lua
  const result = lua.lua_tonumber(L, -1);
  lua.lua_pop(L, 1); // Remove the result from the stack
  return result;
}
// Example usage: Compute the sum of squares for 1 to
1,000,000
const N = 1000000;
console.time("Lua Computation");
const sumOfSquares = calculateSumOfSquares(N);
console.timeEnd("Lua Computation");
console.log(`The sum of squares from 1 to ${N} is:`,
sumOfSquares);
```

In this code, you set up the Lua environment and load the computation function. The **calculateSumOfSquares** function in JavaScript pushes the value of N to the Lua stack, calls the Lua function, and retrieves the result. Notice how you wrap the computation call in **console.time** and **console.timeEnd** to measure its performance.

In addition, when you offload intensive computations to Lua, you'll be amazed at the performance boost you'll see. Lua's interpreter is optimized for speed, so even those big loops or complex algorithms will fly by, faster than if they were in JavaScript. And that means a super responsive user interface for you! All that heavy processing is handled outside of JavaScript's main thread, so you won't have to worry about a thing. Plus, the integration is seamless. All our data is passed between JavaScript and Lua with minimal overhead, so you can do those complex calculations without any delays at all.

This integration not only boosts computational efficiency but also allows you to maintain the interactive features of our JavaScript application, creating a balanced and high-performing web solution.

Summary

To sum up quickly, you developed new skills by combining Lua and JavaScript to make web apps that are more dynamic and run faster. We studied how to use Fengari to connect the two languages so that you could run Lua code in the browser and call Lua functions from JavaScript. We also put Lua scripts inside HTML pages, which showed how dynamic content could be made instantly.

The chapter also talked about how to move and change data between Lua and JavaScript. Additionally, you gained how to give heavy calculations to Lua, which greatly improved the overall performance of our app by leaving JavaScript free to handle user interactions. We saw a full data flow cycle in action, from running Lua code embedded in a web page to getting computed results back in JavaScript. This proved that combining the best features of both languages could create strong and flexible web solutions.

CHAPTER 9: EMBEDDING LUA IN PYTHON APP

Overview

The goal of this chapter is to show you how to easily add Lua to Python programs so that you can use the best features of both languages at the same time. First, you will find out about the different ways that Lua and Python can be linked together. We will hear about binding libraries and interfaces that make it possible for the two languages to talk to each other well. Then, you will pick up the basics of cross-language interoperability so that you can understand how Lua's lightweight scripting features can work with Python's large ecosystem.

The next part will talk about how to embed Lua scripts directly into Python. This will let you run Lua code and send data between the two languages. We can discover how to handle errors in a mixed-language setting, change data structures, and manage runtime environments. This section also talks about useful ways to fix bugs in programs that use both Lua and Python, so you can find problems in both languages. This unified method gives you the tools you need to create strong, fast programs that use Lua's speed and durability while keeping Python's wide range of features.

Bridging Lua and Python

Building on our previous experience with integrating Lua into a JavaScript environment, you discovered that Lua's efficiency and simplicity make it equally suitable for enhancing Python applications. In this topic, you will learn to create a bridge between Lua and Python using Lupa, a powerful binding library that connects these two languages. This integration allows you to offload performance-critical tasks to Lua while leveraging Python's extensive ecosystem for higher-level logic.

We will now practically try out setting up the Lua runtime within Python, executing Lua scripts, and exchanging data between the two environments as below:

Setting up Bridge with Lupa

First run the Lupa which we learned about in the previous chapter. To begin with, at first, import Lupa and initialize a Lua runtime. This Lua state will serve as our embedded interpreter.

```
from lupa import LuaRuntime
# Create a Lua runtime
lua = LuaRuntime(unpack_returned_tuples=True)
```

This simple setup lets you run Lua code from Python.

The **unpack_returned_tuples=True** parameter ensures that Lua functions returning multiple values are handled correctly in Python.

Calculating Factorial

Imagine you have a computationally intensive task, like calculating the factorial of a number. While Python can handle this, Lua's lightweight execution might offer a performance boost for recursive functions.

So here, we define a Lua function for factorial and then call it from Python.

Writing Lua Function

First, define our Lua function as a multi-line string in our Python script:

```
lua_code = """
function factorial(n)
    if n == 0 then
        return 1
    else
        return n * factorial(n - 1)
    end
end
"""
```

Loading and Executing Lua Script

Load this script into the Lua runtime by executing:

```
# Execute the Lua script to load the factorial function
lua.execute(lua_code)
```

Calling Lua Function from Python

Retrieve the Lua function and call it with a sample input:

```
# Retrieve the Lua factorial function
factorial = lua.eval("factorial")
# Compute factorial of 5 using Lua
result = factorial(5)
print("Factorial of 5 is:", result)
```

In this example, the Lua function is invoked from Python just like any Python function. The result returned by Lua is automatically converted to a Python data type, allowing seamless interaction.

Handling Data Exchange between Lua and Python

Data exchange is crucial when combining the strengths of two languages. Lupa automatically converts basic data types between Lua and Python, but you might also need to exchange more complex structures like tables and dictionaries.

Passing Python List to Lua

Suppose you want to process a list of numbers in Lua. We can pass a Python list directly to a Lua function. To understand this better, we extend our previous example by writing a Lua function that computes the sum of the squares of numbers in a table:

```
lua_code_sum = """
function sum_of_squares(numbers)
    local total = 0
    for i = 1, #numbers do
        total = total + numbers[i] * numbers[i]
    end
    return total
end
"""
lua.execute(lua_code_sum)
sum_of_squares = lua.eval("sum_of_squares")
# Define a Python list of numbers
numbers = [2, 3, 4, 5]
# Call the Lua function with the Python list
total = sum_of_squares(numbers)
print("Sum of squares is:", total)
```

Here, the Python list **numbers** is automatically converted to a Lua table, processed by the Lua function, and the result is returned to Python. This demonstrates how seamlessly data can be exchanged between the two environments.

Retrieving Lua Tables as Python Objects

Conversely, if a Lua function returns a table, Lupa converts it to a Python object. For example, let us take an example of a Lua function that creates a user profile:

```
lua_code_profile = """
function create_profile(name, age)
    return {name = name, age = age, interests = {"reading",
"coding", "music"}}
end
"""
lua.execute(lua_code_profile)
create_profile = lua.eval("create_profile")
# Call the Lua function and get a profile
profile = create_profile("Alice", 30)
print("User Profile:", profile)
```

In this case, the returned Lua table is available as a Python dictionary-like object, allowing you to access its keys and values directly.

Debugging Mixed-Language Interactions

I know that bridging Lua and Python is a piece of cake, but I wanted to let you know that there might be a few bumps in the road when it comes to debugging. Sometimes, data doesn't convert as expected, and there might be a few Lua errors. But don't worry! You can use print statements in both languages to inspect values.

For example, if a Lua function fails to execute correctly, Lupa will raise an error in Python that you can catch and log:

```
try:
    faulty_result = lua.eval("non_existent_function")()
except Exception as e:
    print("Caught Lua error:", e)
```

This method allows you to debug mixed-language interactions by tracking down where the data exchange or function call may be failing. The bridge between Lua and Python enabled you to leverage the best of both worlds, enhancing our application's capabilities and opening up new possibilities for performance optimization and innovative problem-solving.

Embedding Lua Scripts in Python

We will now learn to embed Lua scripts directly into our Python application, allowing you to harness Lua's capabilities within our Python projects. Building on our previous learnings around bridging Lua and Python using Lupa, we will now look at practically to loading and executing Lua scripts, and how to call Lua functions from Python. This integration is really great because it makes it so easy for you to incorporate Lua's efficient computation into our Python app. Python will take care of managing the overall application flow and higher-level logic for you.

Loading Lua Script in Python

Here, we first begin with creating a Python file where you will embed our Lua code. Next, we import Lupa and create a Lua state:

```
from lupa import LuaRuntime
# Create a new Lua runtime with tuple unpacking enabled
lua = LuaRuntime(unpack_returned_tuples=True)
```

Next, we then define our Lua script as a multi-line string. For example, we think of a Lua script that contains a function to compute the factorial of a number and a function to generate a greeting message:

```
lua_script = """
function factorial(n)
    if n == 0 then
        return 1
    else
        return n * factorial(n - 1)
    end
end
function greet(name)
    return "Hello, " .. name .. " from Lua!"
end
"""
```

Next, we then load and execute the Lua script in our Python environment:

```
# Load and execute the Lua script
lua.execute(lua_script)
```

At this point, the functions **factorial** and **greet** are available in the Lua runtime, ready to be called from Python.

Calling Lua Functions from Python

To call a Lua function from our Python app, you retrieve the function handle using the **lua.eval** method. For example, to compute the factorial of a number, do the following:

```
# Retrieve the Lua factorial function
factorial = lua.eval("factorial")
# Call the Lua function with an argument (e.g., factorial of
6)
n = 6
fact_result = factorial(n)
print(f"The factorial of {n} is: {fact_result}")
```

Similarly, you can call the **greet** function:

```
# Retrieve the Lua greet function
greet = lua.eval("greet")
# Call the greet function with a sample name
name = "Alice"
greeting = greet(name)
print(greeting)
```

This shows how easily you can invoke Lua functions from Python. The Lua code runs within its own runtime, processes the input, and returns the result back to our Python program.

Exchanging Data between Python and Lua

The basic data types like numbers, strings, and lists are automatically converted between the two languages. To understand it practically, let us consider a Lua function that sums the squares of a list of numbers.

Here, we first define the Lua function as follows:

```
lua_code_sum = """
function sum_of_squares(numbers)
    local total = 0
    for i = 1, #numbers do
        total = total + numbers[i] * numbers[i]
    end
    return total
end
"""
lua.execute(lua_code_sum)
```

Next, retrieve and call this function from Python, passing a Python list as the argument:

```
# Retrieve the Lua function
sum_of_squares = lua.eval("sum_of_squares")
# Create a Python list of numbers
numbers = [2, 3, 4, 5]
# Call the Lua function with the Python list
result = sum_of_squares(numbers)
print("Sum of squares:", result)
```

The Lupa automatically converts the Python list into a Lua table. The Lua function processes the table, calculates the sum of squares, and the result is returned to Python as a number.

Embedding Complex Scripts

You can embed more complex Lua scripts to perform all sorts of tasks, like data transformation, mathematical computations, or even custom business logic. For example, say you have a Lua script that processes user data and returns a structured result.

Below is how we defined the Lua script:

```
lua_script_data = """
function process_user_data(user)
```

```
    local processed = {}
    processed.username = user.username:upper()
    processed.age = user.age + 5  -- Example transformation
    processed.interests = {}
    for i, interest in ipairs(user.interests) do
        processed.interests[i] = interest:sub(1,1):upper() ..
interest:sub(2)
    end
    return processed
end
"""
lua.execute(lua_script_data)
```

In Python, create a dictionary to represent the user and pass it to the Lua function:

```
# Retrieve the Lua function for processing user data
process_user_data = lua.eval("process_user_data")
# Create a Python dictionary representing a user
user_data = {
    'username': 'alice',
    'age': 25,
    'interests': ['reading', 'cycling', 'coding']
}
# Call the Lua function with the user data
processed_user = process_user_data(user_data)
print("Processed User Data:")
print("Username:", processed_user['username'])
print("Age:", processed_user['age'])
print("Interests:", processed_user['interests'])
```

Lupa then automatically converts the Python dictionary into a Lua table and vice versa. The Lua function processes the data—converting the username to uppercase, incrementing the age, and capitalizing each interest—then returns a new table that becomes a Python dictionary. Throughout this demonstration, you actively embedded Lua scripts into our Python application, executed Lua code, and exchanged data between the two environments.

Interoperability and Data Exchange

Converting Basic Data Types

When you pass data from Python to Lua using Lupa, basic types are automatically converted. For example, Python numbers, strings, and booleans become their Lua equivalents without any manual intervention. Similarly, when Lua returns values to Python, Lupa converts them back into native Python types.

Let us do a simple exercise wherein you create a Python variable and pass it to a Lua function that performs a calculation, and then retrieve the result.

```
from lupa import LuaRuntime
lua = LuaRuntime(unpack_returned_tuples=True)
# Lua function for a simple arithmetic operation
lua.execute('''
function add_numbers(a, b)
    return a + b
end
''')
# Retrieve the Lua function and call it with Python numbers
add_numbers = lua.eval("add_numbers")
result = add_numbers(10, 20)
print("Result of addition:", result)  # Expected output: 30
```

Here, the Python numbers 10 and 20 are automatically converted to Lua numbers, and the result is then converted back to a Python number.

Handling Complex Data Structures

The true power of interoperability comes into play when exchanging complex data structures. Python lists become Lua tables and Python dictionaries become Lua tables with key-value pairs. For instance, if you want to process a list of values or a dictionary representing user data, Lupa takes care of the conversion so that you can work with them naturally in Lua.

Example 1: Converting a Python List

Let us say that we have a Python list of integers that you want to sum in Lua. Here, the Lupa automatically converts the list to a Lua table when passed as an argument.

```
lua_code = '''
function sum_list(numbers)
    local total = 0
    for i = 1, #numbers do
        total = total + numbers[i]
    end
    return total
end
'''
lua.execute(lua_code)
sum_list = lua.eval("sum_list")
numbers = [1, 2, 3, 4, 5]
total = sum_list(numbers)
print("Sum of list:", total)  # Expected output: 15
```

Here, the Python list **`numbers`** is converted to a Lua table, processed by the Lua function, and the result is returned as a Python number.

Example 2: Exchanging a Dictionary

Similarly, if you have a Python dictionary with multiple fields, it is automatically converted into a Lua table. Try an example wherein we have a function that processes user profile data:

```
lua_code_profile = '''
function process_profile(profile)
    profile.username = profile.username:upper()
    profile.age = profile.age + 1
    return profile
```

```
end
'''
lua.execute(lua_code_profile)
process_profile = lua.eval("process_profile")
user_profile = {
    'username': 'alice',
    'age': 25,
    'interests': ['reading', 'cycling', 'coding']
}
processed_profile = process_profile(user_profile)
print("Processed Profile:", processed_profile)
```

In this example, the Python dictionary **user_profile** is passed to Lua. The Lua function modifies the **username** by converting it to uppercase and increments the **age**. The updated table is then converted back to a Python dictionary.

Synchronizing State across Boundaries

Synchronizing state means that you can modify data in Lua and see those changes reflected in Python, and vice versa. When you pass mutable objects like dictionaries or lists, the state is maintained across the call boundary, allowing you to use Lua to perform in-place updates on Python data structures. For example, if you modify a table in Lua that was originally a Python list, you can continue to use that list in Python with the changes applied.

To understand better, let us try out an example where you want to update a list of values based on some computation:

```
lua_code_update = '''
function update_values(numbers)
    for i = 1, #numbers do
        numbers[i] = numbers[i] * 2
    end
    return numbers
end
'''
```

```
lua.execute(lua_code_update)
update_values = lua.eval("update_values")
data = [10, 20, 30]
updated_data = update_values(data)
print("Updated Data:", updated_data)  # Expected output: [20,
40, 60]
```

Here, the list **data** is modified in Lua and then returned. The Python variable **updated_data** reflects the updated values.

Advanced Data Exchange Techniques

Lupa handles nested lists and dictionaries recursively, so you can pass complex objects without having to manually flatten or reassemble them. For example, if you have a nested data structure representing orders and items, Lua can traverse and update the nested tables, and the entire structure will be returned intact to Python.

```
lua_code_nested = '''
function process_orders(orders)
    for _, order in ipairs(orders) do
        for i, item in ipairs(order.items) do
            order.items[i] = item * 1.1  -- apply a 10%
increase to each item price
        end
    end
    return orders
end
'''
lua.execute(lua_code_nested)
process_orders = lua.eval("process_orders")
orders = [
    {'order_id': 101, 'items': [100, 200, 300]},
    {'order_id': 102, 'items': [150, 250]}
]
```

```
processed_orders = process_orders(orders)
print("Processed Orders:", processed_orders)
```

In this example, a list of orders (each with an **order_id** and a list of **items**) is passed to Lua. The Lua function applies a 10% increase to each item price and returns the updated list. Python then receives the updated data structure, with all nested elements converted correctly.

While Lupa does a great job of automatically converting types, there might be cases where you need to ensure that the data meets specific formats or constraints. We can incorporate error checking within our Lua functions to validate data before processing. For example, you might add a check in our Lua function to verify that all elements in a table are numbers before performing arithmetic operations. Any discrepancies can be handled within Lua, or an error message can be returned to Python for further handling.

Debugging Lua-Python Applications

You might run into errors related to data conversion, function calls, or unexpected behavior in the Lua runtime when building applications that use both languages. So, if you want to be able to track down issues quickly and maintain a solid codebase, you should learn to debug these mixed-language applications.

Capturing and Logging Lua Errors

One common issue is that Lua functions might fail due to syntax errors or runtime problems, and these errors can propagate into our Python application. With Lupa, you can catch these errors using Python's exception handling mechanisms. For example, suppose you try to execute a Lua script that contains an error. We can wrap the call in a try-except block to capture and log the error message.

```
from lupa import LuaRuntime
lua = LuaRuntime(unpack_returned_tuples=True)
# Define a faulty Lua script with an error (missing 'end' in
function)
faulty_lua_script = """
function faulty_function(n)
    if n > 0 then
        return n * 2
    -- Missing 'end' here causes a syntax error
```

```
"""
try:
    lua.execute(faulty_lua_script)
except Exception as e:
    print("Caught Lua error during script execution:", e)
```

In this example, the missing **end** leads to a Lua syntax error. When you run this, Python catches the exception and prints an error message. This approach lets you isolate and correct issues in our Lua code without crashing our Python application.

Debugging Function Calls and Data Conversion

Another common issue arises from the automatic conversion of data types between Python and Lua. Sometimes, the data may not convert as expected, or the Lua function might return a type that is not compatible with our Python code. We can debug these issues by checking the data types at various points.

For example, think of a Lua function that should return a number, but instead returns nil due to an error in computation.

```
lua_script = """
function compute_value(x)
    if x < 0 then
        return nil   -- Unexpected nil for negative numbers
    else
        return x * 10
    end
end
"""
lua.execute(lua_script)
compute_value = lua.eval("compute_value")
# Debug function call with a negative value
result = compute_value(-5)
if result is None:
    print("Debug: Received None when computing value for -5")
```

```
else:
    print("Computed value:", result)
```

In this case, you see that passing a negative number returns **`None`**, allowing you to handle this case explicitly in our Python code.

Inspecting Lua State and Stack Contents

Sometimes, you need to examine the Lua state directly to understand what values are on the stack or how the functions are being called. Lupa provides access to some of the Lua API, so you can print stack contents or check global variables.

For example, if a Lua function does not seem to be available, you can verify its existence by querying the Lua global environment.

```
# Check if the function 'greet' exists in the Lua global table
lua_script_greet = """
function greet(name)
    return "Hello, " .. name
end
"""
lua.execute(lua_script_greet)
# Retrieve the 'greet' function
greet_function = lua.eval("greet")
if greet_function is None:
    print("Debug: 'greet' function not found in Lua globals")
else:
    print("Debug: 'greet' function successfully loaded")
```

In the above, it confirms that the Lua function **`greet`** is properly defined and available. If it is not found, you know to check the Lua script or the loading process.

Debugging Data Exchange Issues

There are also issues that can pop up when you're dealing with complex data structures, like nested dictionaries or lists. To figure out what's going on, you might want to print the data on both the Lua and Python sides.

For example, if you pass a Python dictionary to Lua and then tweak it, you can print the resulting structure in Lua before returning it.

```
lua_script_data = """
function process_data(data)
    -- Print the received data for debugging purposes
    for key, value in pairs(data) do
        print("Lua debug:", key, value)
    end
    -- Modify data: add a new key-value pair
    data.processed = true
    return data
end
"""
lua.execute(lua_script_data)
process_data = lua.eval("process_data")
# Create a Python dictionary to send to Lua
sample_data = {"name": "Bob", "age": 30}
processed_data = process_data(sample_data)
print("Processed Data in Python:", processed_data)
```

In this case, the Lua function prints each key-value pair it receives. We then check in our Python console that the returned dictionary includes the new key, **`processed`**, set to **`true`**. This immediate feedback helps you ensure that the data exchange and modifications occur as expected.

Try-Except Blocks for Mixed-Language Debugging

A great trick for debugging code that uses different languages is to use try-except blocks in Python around our Lua function calls. This can help find problems during both Lua execution and when you're converting data.

To give you an idea, following is a quick example:

```
lua_script_error = """
function divide(a, b)
```

```
    if b == 0 then
        error("Division by zero")
    end
    return a / b
end
"""
lua.execute(lua_script_error)
divide = lua.eval("divide")
try:
    # This will trigger an error due to division by zero
    result = divide(10, 0)
    print("Division Result:", result)
except Exception as e:
    print("Caught error during division:", e)
```

In this, you can prevent our Python application from crashing and log detailed error messages for further investigation. This method is for identifying logical errors and ensuring robustness of our mixed-language application.

Debugging Complex Interactions

When our Python application becomes more complex, with multiple Lua functions and data exchanges happening concurrently, debugging can involve tracking the flow of data through various components. In such cases, consider logging intermediate values and states on both the Lua and Python sides. We might write a small utility function in Lua that logs information to a file, then call this function from Python whenever you need to trace execution.

```
-- Lua script for logging debug information
function log_debug(message)
    local file = io.open("debug.log", "a")
    if file then
        file:write(os.date("%Y-%m-%d %H:%M:%S") .. " - " ..
message .. "\n")
        file:close()
```

```
    end
end
```

Then, from Python, you can call this logging function before and after critical Lua function calls:

```
log_debug = lua.eval("log_debug")
log_debug("Starting complex computation...")
# Call a complex Lua function
complex_function = lua.eval("complex_function")
try:
    result = complex_function()
    print("Complex function result:", result)
except Exception as e:
    print("Error in complex function:", e)
log_debug("Completed complex computation.")
```

And the best part is that it keeps a record of everything that's happened, which is super handy when you're dealing with issues in production.

Summary

To sum up, you used the Lupa library to add Lua to Python programs, showing that the two languages can work together without any problems. We studied to set up a Lua runtime in Python and run Lua scripts directly from Python, calling Lua functions to do things like find factorials and work with user data. We practiced sending computations that are very important to performance to Lua while keeping Python's many features for logic at a higher level.

You saw that Lua's short syntax and fast execution worked well with Python's large library, which made the whole application run faster. We also took care of more complicated data structures by moving nested objects between the two environments and making sure that the states were correctly synchronized. We used debugging tools like try-except blocks and logging to find errors and look at the Lua state when problems arose, which helped you solve mixed-language issues successfully. We were able to make strong, fast, mixed-language apps that used the best features of both Lua and Python by mastering these interoperability methods. This chapter and the one before it made it much easier for you to make and keep up-to-date complex multilingual solutions.

Index

M

N

O

P

R

S

T

U

V

W

Epilogue

In light of everything we've covered thus far in Practical Lua 5 Programming, I can't wait to see what the future holds. The knowledge and abilities we have discussed will help you to build a strong basis from which to take use of Lua's unique features: speed, simplicity, and light weight design. These qualities make Lua a great choice for embedded devices and applications where resources are few. Over all of this, you have perfected building effective Lua scripts, precisely managing data, and combining Lua with languages including JavaScript and Python.

Within the realm of embedded devices, where every byte of memory and every millisecond of processing time counts, Lua's low impact is evident. Whether it's scripting firmware, automating IoT devices, or applying control logic in industrial systems, the practical examples you have worked through have equipped you to handle real-world problems. Lua's flawless interaction with C and other low-level languages lets you include its interpreter into bespoke hardware solutions, therefore providing flexibility without sacrificing speed.

From file handling and data processing to sophisticated tools like coroutines and metatables, the methods you have learned fit Lua's effective running speed. Whether your job involves smart home devices, network routers, or mobile devices, these tools let you create apps that shine in performance and adaptability. Using Lua in your embedded projects will help you better handle resources, delegate difficult calculations, and make sure that your projects are responsive in all situations.

This is only the beginning. Your acquired expertise serves as a launching pad for creativity, enabling you to investigate Lua's possibilities as the pillar of high-performance, adaptable embedded space applications. I urge you to experiment, innovate, and challenge the boundaries of what's feasible with Lua going ahead. Your practical knowledge opens a universe of possibilities whereby your creativity can transform daily problems into dependable, scalable, and quick answers.

The road keeps on and the opportunities are almost endless.

Thank You

www.ingramcontent.com/pod-product-compliance
Lightning Source LLC
Chambersburg PA
CBHW080214170726
48282CB00030B/1118
9788198431660